Relevant Reading

Investigating Historical Documents in Today's World

by Delana Heidrich

illustrated by Kathryn Marlin

cover by Don Ellens

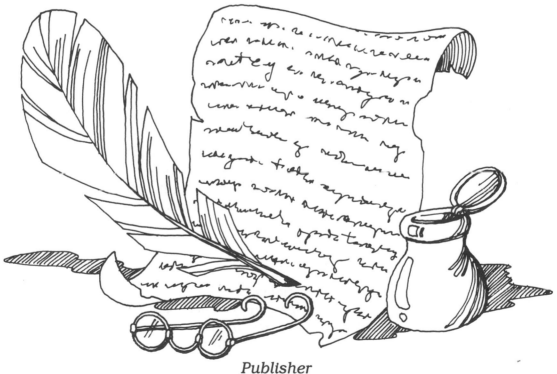

Publisher
Instructional Fair • TS Denison
Grand Rapids, Michigan 49544

ISBN: 1-56822-848-1

Relevant Reading: Investigating Historical Documents in Today's World
Copyright © 1999 by Ideal • Instructional Fair Publishing Group
a division of Tribune Education
2400 Turner Avenue NW
Grand Rapids, Michigan 49544

Table of Contents

Introduction

Throughout history, political documents have been drawn up, debated, signed, revised, thrown out, and drawn up again in ceaseless attempts to define the relationship between state and individual rights and responsibilities that best maintain social order. Unrestricted individual liberties create chaos while unrestricted state powers squelch human spirit and often bring outright rebellion. The ideal balance is forever being redefined through discussions in classrooms, deliberations in courtrooms, and debates on senate floors.

Relevant Reading: Investigating Historical Documents in Today's World brings to life monumental acts, proclamations, charters, and agreements from around the world as it explores the historical context and modern-day significance of the Magna Carta, the United States Constitution, and nine other famous documents through Web pages, speeches, lecture reviews, and other real-world readings. Well-defined student activities and extension projects enrich the readings by encouraging critical thinking and providing supplemental information, while thorough background material and an extensive answer key provide the instructor with easily referenced knowledge about each document.

Each of the 11 chapters presented here in chronological order constitutes a complete unit of study on a separate, famous document from history. The Code of Hammurabi—the earliest known complete set of laws—is compared and contrasted with our nation's present system of justice. Constitutional monarchies are examined in a chapter addressing the Magna Carta. Lesser-known historical details surrounding the writings of the Declaration of Independence, the United States Constitution, and the Bill of Rights contextualize these famous documents for readers. The issues of slavery and the American Civil War are addressed in the chapter on the Emancipation Proclamation. The chapters on the Communist Manifesto and New Deal Legislation examine social issues within past and present cultures. And the chapters on the United Nations Charter, the Civil Rights Act of 1964, and the 1992 Earth Summit Agreements all anticipate a future of global cooperativeness. Distribute each unit in its entirety as a single student packet or choose readings and activities to supplement your history, social studies, or language arts textbook.

The Code of Hammurabi

When Hammurabi, king of Babylon from 1792 to 1750 B.C., codified laws governing everything from business practices to criminal punishments, he had them carved into stone along with long-winded curses on any subsequent ruler who might decide to alter them. Claiming that his authority to "rule over men" and "enlighten the land" came from Shamash, the god of justice, Hammurabi included in his code protections for the weak and equal retaliation punishments for the guilty. The Code of Hammurabi is the world's oldest known nearly complete set of laws, and, as such, has influenced countless legal systems throughout the ages.

Hammurabi's Code consists of 282 individual statutes addressing farmer-worker relations, merchant-buyer relations, service fee schedules, family law, legal procedures, and forms of punishment. Although some of the rules and punishments may seem to modern people arbitrary or unfair, Hammurabi believed he had been called by the gods to "cause justice to prevail in the land, to destroy the wicked and the evil." In an epilogue to the code, he described his statutes as "laws of justice . . . a righteous law and pious statute." He stressed that his words were "well considered" and his deeds "not equaled." "There is not wisdom like unto mine," he claimed.

An investigation of this ancient code can provide the "big picture" for students who witness America questioning the effectiveness of its own justice system. Did Hammurabi's Code include anything resembling California's "three strikes and you're out" policy? Does inflicting floggings as punishment, as proposed by some in American society today, have a historical counterpart in the Code? Did Hammurabi demonstrate any of the principles of restorative justice as advocated by Equal Justice USA, Campaign of Equity Restorative Justice, and other organizations?

In this lesson, students compare and contrast Hammurabi's Code with today's legal system and investigate the differences between justice as restoration and as retribution as they read an imaginary pamphlet circulated by Restorative Justice advocates.

Victim Rights

Students answer critical thinking questions based on the student reading.

Crime and Punishment

Students consider how the breaking of school rules might be punished if punishments were to follow the example of Hammurabi's Code.

1. Sharpen your Internet skills by locating the facts and verdicts of famous historical and recent court cases in the United States. Require each student to report on one case that seemed justly decided and one that did not.

2. As a class read Hammurabi's Code of Laws in its entirety or assign the reading and reporting on specific sections to individual groups of students. The code can be located on the Internet at the Yahoo site entitled "Exploring Ancient World Cultures: Readings from the Ancient Near East." Ask students whether the Code provides any historical counterpart for California's "three strikes and you're out" policy, the idea of flogging, or the ideas of restorative justice (Answer: No, in the first two instances, yes in the third).

3. Hammurabi was not only a great ruler, but also a remarkable warrior who united the entire Mesopotamian region through numerous battles. Research the life and times of King Hammurabi in the "cradle of civilization" now known as Iraq.

4. Learn about the United States' judicial system. Visit a courtroom. Invite an attorney or judge to speak to your class. Read Article III of the Constitution. Clip and post articles about justice and justice reform movements in the United States.

VICTIMS IN THE COURTROOM

Your Legal Rights

As a recent victim of a nonviolent crime, you join hundreds of thousands of other innocent people whose rights and property have been violated by a fellow human being. How you respond to your situation is a personal decision. If you choose to be involved in the entire justice process, Restorative Justice activists can support your choice.

Restorative Justice activists campaign for a form of justice that requires criminals to be accountable for their crimes yet provides victims with restitution and restored feelings of safety. The idea is not a new one. The world's oldest known legal code, Hammurabi's Code of Laws, was intended to "bring about the well-being of the oppressed." Individuals who were stolen from, cheated, or mistreated were repaid. The man who "took from the granary or box [corn or money] without the knowledge of the owner" did not spend a year in prison—he "repaid the corn he had taken."

Although many of the punishments included in the code would seem harsh by modern standards, they did fit the crime. If a son were to strike his father, his hand would be cut off. If a man knocked the teeth out of another, his own teeth would be knocked out. Restorative Justice does not advocate violence, but the principle of a punishment fitting the crime is one its members support. Proponents would say, "Let the graffiti 'artist' wash walls and clean city streets for six months and let the thief repay his victim with money or labor instead of throwing the offenders into expensive prisons, never having had to face their victims or restore what they have destroyed or stolen."

The U.S. prison population has tripled since the 1980s and 84 percent of the increase can be attributed to nonviolent offenses, according to a National Center on Institutions and Alternatives report. Prison terms isolate offenders from their communities. This does not promote community healing following a crime, nor does it prevent crime in the community in the future.

As a victim, you have a right to live in a community that holds its offenders accountable. You have a right to confront your offender. You have a right to tell your offender what damage he or she has caused and to request repayment. You have a right to band with your fellow community members to address the underlying causes of crime in your area so that you can feel safe, not just until your personal offender gets out of prison, but throughout your lifetime. Plus you have an obligation to address the physical, psychological, and moral needs of the young in your community, to address the causes of crime in your area, and to offer education and support to offenders who make the conscious choice to rejoin the community as active, productive, and civil citizens.

Hammurabi lived in a very different time in history (nearly 1,800 years before Christ) when slavery was condoned and violent and physical sentences accompanied offenses against society; but he well understood that a crime is not only the breaking of a rule, it is also the destruction of a relationship with other people affecting the entire community. Hammurabi outlined 282 specific situations that arose in Mesopotamian life and required legal resolution. He tackled problems of family relations, merchant-buyer agreements, prison conditions, farmer-worker relations, theft, inheritance, fee schedules, and numerous other legal issues. With each statute, he acknowledged the need for offenders to be accountable for their deeds, the strong not to injure the weak, and "the well-being of mankind" to be furthered. Four thousand years later, could we not at least do the same?

Restorative justice advocates urge you to be actively involved in the justice system. Face your offender. Request restitution. Offer support to offenders who wish to reenter society as fruitful members. And address poverty, drug abuse, and other underlying causes of future crime.

Victim Rights

On your own paper, answer the following questions, which are based on the student reading, in complete sentences.

1. Restorative Justice advocates contend that today's legal system relies on "retributive justice," which focuses on punishment and vengeance. How does retributive justice differ from restorative justice? Why do restorative justice advocates believe their approach to be the better of the two when dealing with crime? Which approach do you support?

2. Hammurabi believed he was bringing the people laws given him by ancient gods. Are there other codes of conduct or laws that claim divine origin? What gives U.S. laws their authority?

3. Hammurabi included safeguards in his laws pertaining to judicial procedures to assure that individuals were not unjustly accused or convicted. For example, if a man were to bring "an accusation of any crime before the elders, and does not prove what he has charged," the accuser would receive the punishment. Likewise, if a judge were to judge in error, he would pay 12 times the fine he imposed and be removed from the judge's seat. What safeguards does the United States judicial system reserve for the accused?

4. Many of Hammurabi's laws pertaining to service required an individual who was hired to do a job to pay five or more times the "damages" when a job was not done properly. A physician who killed a man in performing an operation even lost his hands! How do these service laws correspond to today's small claims courts and professional malpractice insurance and liability suits?

Crime and Punishment

How would student offenses be punished at school if Hammurabi wrote a Code of School Rules? Read the following Hammurabi rules and determine a similar punishment to the broken school rule listed beside it in the "Crime" column.

Hammurabi Law	Crime	Punishment
If a builder builds a house for someone, and does not construct it properly, and the house which he built falls in and kills its owner, then that builder shall be put to death.	You pay your school a locker fee. However, the lock is broken and all your belongings are stolen.	
If anyone steals a plow, he shall pay three shekels in money.	You steal a classmate's new backpack.	
If a herdsman, to whose care cattle are entrusted . . . sells them for money . . . he shall pay the owner ten times the loss.	Your teammate asks you to watch his warm-up jacket. You let your girlfriend wear it, and she loses it.	
If anyone hires an ox or an ass, and a lion kills it in the field, the loss is upon its owner.	You lend your calculator to a friend and the battery dies while he is using it.	
If a man hires an ox, and he breaks its leg . . . he shall compensate the owner with ox for ox.	You spill soup on a book you have borrowed from the library.	
If a man breaks another man's bone, his bone shall be broken.	You get in a fist fight and give a classmate a nosebleed.	
If a free man strikes the body of another free man, he shall pay one gold mina.	You punch an opponent out of anger while playing basketball.	
If anyone brings accusation before the elders and does not prove what he has charged . . . , he shall receive the fine that the action produces.	You falsely accuse a classmate of cheating on a test.	

The Magna Carta

Background

Monarchy is a form of government dating back 5,000 years, but the monarchies of today do not resemble those of yesteryear very much—thanks in part to English barons, knights, and bishops who in 1215 strong-armed King John into granting the Magna Carta—the first charter that limited the powers of sovereigns.

Eleventh- and twelfth-century England operated under the political system known as *feudalism*. The king granted land to barons who granted land to knights who granted land to other vassals all in exchange for allegiance and military and agricultural services. By the 1200s King John had gained so much clout under this hierarchical system that his rampant abuses of power provoked barons to storm the castle and demand the king sign a charter specifying citizen rights and assuring that King John himself would live under the law. The charter not only abolished abuses by the crown but also contained the first definition of king-baron relations as well as protections of international trade, a system of standard weights and measures, rules for conducting trials, and standardized penalties for felonies.

The limiting of the powers of kings that began with the signing of the Magna Carta and culminated with the Glorious Revolution in 1688 and the reign of William III and Mary II set a precedent for the world. Constitutional monarchies today boast elected representatives, constitutions, parliaments, and strong democracies. Great Britain, Norway, Sweden, Canada, Japan, Spain, and Denmark are all constitutional monarchies. The days of unchallengeable authority as a royal birthright are over.

Proponents of this popular form of modern government claim that constitutional monarchies include the best of both worlds—an elected head of government who sets policy and "runs" the government and a ceremonial head of state who serves as a symbol of national unity. Supporters speak of heritage and history and tradition and steadfastness in governments that retain a sovereign power.

Yet not all citizens of such countries support the system. In Canada and Australia, citizen groups are campaigning to abolish the monarchy and create a republic. In Great Britain resentment of royal embarrassments is epidemic. Supporters of the republic movements in these countries claim that the monarchy is an antiquated system of government that has no place in today's world. They point to the symbolic nature of monarchs, the illogic of the assumption that heredity makes one a fine ruler, the problems created when royalty divorce, and the unrealistic standards monarchs are expected to live by in a world where secrets inevitably become public.

In this lesson students examine the Magna Carta and learn about past and present monarchies as they review the web site of a fictitious historical society. Through student activities they formulate their own opinions about the effectiveness of constitutional monarchies, explore the similarities and differences among various forms of government, and write modern language interpretations of the Magna Carta.

Teaching Activities

Long Live the Queen

Students decide for themselves if constitutional monarchies create stable, effective democracies as they answer these questions based on the student reading.

The Great Charter

Students interpret the Magna Carta (Latin for *the Great Charter*) based on the history highlighted in the student reading.

Presidents, Sultans, Tyrants, and Queens

Students explore the similarities and differences between various forms of government as they match rulers to their governments.

1. Locate web sites of supporters of the monarchy and of the movement to create a republic in Canada as well as in Australia. Conduct a class debate on the pros and cons of abolishing the monarchies and creating republics in the two countries.

2. The history of constitutional monarchies varies from country to country. While England has enjoyed democracy since the 1600s when James II was overthrown and the Declaration of Rights was accepted by William III and Mary II, Spain did not adopt a national constitution until 1978. Divide the class into several groups and require each group to research and report on the history and present-day workings of a constitutional monarchy (i.e., Great Britain, Thailand, Japan, the Netherlands, Norway, Sweden, Denmark, Spain, Australia, Canada, New Zealand, Portugal). How do the Parliamentarian systems differ from country to country? In which country does royalty maintain the most power? The most symbolic prestige? What is the title for sovereignty in each country (sultan, king, emperor, czar, kaiser)? Which countries are commonwealths of Great Britain, presided over by a governor general who represents Queen Elizabeth II, and which claim their own monarch?

3. Despotic regimes can be found among republics as well as among monarchies. Research the differences between a constitutional monarchy and a republic. How are distinctions made between various forms of government? Study and report on Aristotle's system for classifying states, a system that continues to influence political thought today.

4. Research and report on the people and events that transformed the absolute powers of ancient monarchies into the constitutional monarchies of today. Be certain to explore the stories of Stephan Langton, archbishop of Canterbury at the time of the granting of the Magna Carta, and the Glorious Revolution in England during the seventeenth century.

WELCOME TO THE HOME PAGE OF
THE GLOBAL GOVERNMENTS HISTORICAL SOCIETY

To learn more about monarchies, click an italicized title:

A History of Monarchies
The Magna Carta
Constitutional Monarchies
A Modern Debate

A History of Monarchies

Monarchy is a form of government in which a single person serves as the head of state of a nation for his or her lifetime based on heredity. In ancient societies, monarchs enjoyed absolute power because they were believed to be God's divine representatives. This political authority continued for European monarchs during the Middle Ages because the feudal system depended on a hierarchy of allegiance and military service that placed the king at the top. When King James abused his powers by issuing arbitrary fines, taxations, and punishments, barons in England demanded he sign the Magna Carta—the first charter that limited the power of sovereigns. In the seventeenth century when King James II was overthrown and William III and Mary II took over the throne and affirmed the Bill of Rights, the supremacy of Parliament over the Crown was solidified. Today monarchies throughout the world are constitutional. Parliaments are composed of representatives of the people under the law, and an elected head of government enjoys a great deal more real power than the hereditary head of state. Constitutional monarchies are democratic nations in which the legislative bodies and the prime minister govern, and the sovereign is a figurehead who symbolizes the nation's unity.

The Magna Carta

In 1215 English barons who complained that King John demanded more overseas military duties than was fair, intimidated subjects into loyalty, and forced barons and knights to pay unfair fees and taxes demanded that the king sign the Magna Carta—a charter that guaranteed the freedom of the church and certain citizen liberties. Principle tenets of the Magna Carta include the independence of the English church, the rights of inheritance, the prohibition of the unlawful seizure of land, the freedom of trade, and fixed laws defining fair taxes and duties of barons and knights.

The Magna Carta was confirmed by Parliament in 1216, modified numerous times, and supported by the Petition of Rights in 1628 and the Bill of Rights in 1689. It served as a springboard for rebels in the seventeenth century who assured once and for all the supremacy of Parliament over the monarch during the Glorious Revolution. Although it may be refuted by Parliament at any time, the Magna Carta has been in force for over 700 years.

A Modern Debate

Citizens of some constitutional monarchies today would like to be rid of royalty. Most notably, citizen groups in Canada and Australia, hope to revise their constitutions to dissolve the monarchy and establish republic states. Supporters of the republic movement claim that monarchies are antiquated forms of government, while those who wish to continue in their present system point to the numerous modern constitutional monarchies that maintain stable, economically sound democracies worldwide. As Canada and Australia are both commonwealths of England, republic supporters in both countries can also claim that allegiance to a nation so distant from their own shores serves little purpose at home.

Regardless of the controversies in Canada and Australia, the system of constitutional monarchy which owes its existence to the limits of sovereign powers initiated with the signing of the Magna Carta in 1215, proves to be a sound political system in nations as diverse as Japan and Belgium or Norway and the Netherlands. In fact, the United Nations' 1995 listing of the ten best countries in which to live based on standard of living and political freedom included six constitutional monarchies. Long live the constitutional monarchy!

Constitutional Monarchies

Monarchies of the modern world take the form of constitutional monarchies that claim both a head of state (a queen, king, emperor, or other sovereign) and a head of government (often titled prime minister). The prime minister is elected by the people in some countries and appointed by the sovereign in others. All constitutional monarchies maintain some form of elected representation in government, usually in the form of a parliament. The sovereign is bound by a constitution to approve all bills passed by the parliament. Likewise, the sovereign is required to live under the same laws as are the citizens of the constitutional monarchy. Although sovereigns claim varying degrees of power from country to country, the king or queen in most modern constitutional monarchies is a symbolic position, serving to unify the nation and provide a national identity. The Queen of England, for example, officially opens Parliament with an address drafted by the prime minister and his representatives rather than by her own "team." Although she is consulted about many issues, other individuals (some elected and some appointed) oversee the day-to-day operations of governing in her name.

Click on an italicized heading to:

Return to Historical Society Home page
Review the Magna Carta
Review a Modern Debate

Review a History of Monarchies
Review Constitutional Monarchies
Go on to Student Activities

Long Live the Queen

Answer the following questions about monarchies based on the student reading of The Global Governments Historical Society's Home Page.

1. The feudal system of the Middle Ages in Europe was necessary as a king needed to rely on the barons and knights below him to provide military service and allegiance in a world in which regions were constantly at war with one another. Although their powers have been limited, why do you think monarchs continue to exist in a world where nations cooperate and trade in relative peace and nationalized military systems have been established to fight wars when necessary?

2. At the time of the writing of the Magna Carta, men lost jobs and lives for speaking their minds. The king held absolute power and could demand you pay him money, give him (or his representatives) grains from your land, or complete overseas military service in his name at any time. What might have given the barons of 1215 the courage to stand up to King John? Could you have done so?

3. Some supporters of a monarchical system claim that having the head of state and the head of government being two separate people frees the head of government to govern without worrying about image because he or she does not symbolize national unity, while it allows the country to maintain a strong national identity by having a symbolic head of state. Is this a better system than a republic in which a single president must be "governor" and "symbol" of the nation? Why or why not?

4. England's constitution is not a single, difficult-to-modify document, but rather a list of laws, customs, and court decisions. What are the advantages and disadvantages of having a constant, hard-to-change document serve as the constitution as does the United States?

The Great Charter

According to the student reading, the Magna Carta was presented to King John by barons who were angry with his abuses of power. Even though the feudal system under which King John ruled no longer exists in England or elsewhere, many of the tenets of the Magna Carta serve to limit the powers of monarchs today. Translate the following Magna Carta phrases into modern-day language. Be advised that the words "we" and "our" refer to the king. Although barons, knights, and bishops wrote the charter, it was granted by King John, who was forced to sign it by threat of rebellion by his subjects.

1. "No constable or other bailiff of ours shall take corn or other provisions from anyone without immediately tendering money thereof . . ."
   Interpretation:

2. "All merchants shall have safe and secure exit from England, and entry to England, with a right to tarry there . . ."
   Interpretation:

3. "No scutage nor aid shall be imposed on our kingdom, unless by common counsel of our kingdom . . ."
   Interpretation:

4. "No freeman shall be taken or imprisoned . . . except by the lawful judgment of his peers, or by the law of the land."
   Interpretation:

5. "A freeman shall not be amerced for a slight offense, except in accordance with the degree of the offense."
   Interpretation:

6. "No one shall be distrained for performance of greater service for a knight's fee, or for any other free tenement, than is due there from."
   Interpretation:

7. "Common pleas shall not follow our court, but shall be held in some fixed place."
   Interpretation:

Presidents, Sultans, Tyrants, and Queens

Types of government overlap and cannot easily be defined, but some terms (many originating with Aristotle) have stood the test of time. In Part A match the forms of government listed on the left with their descriptions on the right. In Part B match the rulers on the left with the forms of government within which they operate on the right.

Part A

1. _____ Monarchy

2. _____ Constitutional Monarchy

3. _____ Oligarchy

4. _____ Democracy

5. _____ Republic

6. _____ Dictatorship

Part B

7. _____ President

8. _____ King, Sultan, Emperor, Czar

9. _____ Prime Minister

10. _____ Dictator

a. a government that does not have a monarch; usually a representative, democratic system, but not always

b. government by a few people

c. government with a single hereditary head of state who rules for life

d. a monarchy in which the monarch has limited powers and must live under the law

e. a government in which the supreme power is held by the people

f. a twentieth-century government in which a single person, often a military leader, holds all power

g. all different words for monarch or head of state

h. the leader of a dictatorship

i. the leader of a democratic republic

j. the head of government in a constitutional monarchy

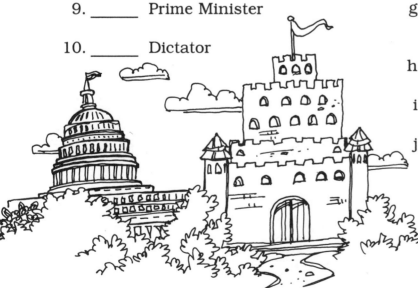

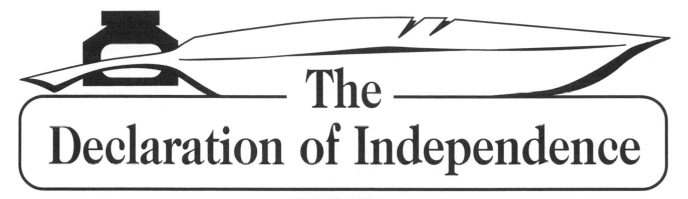

The
Declaration of Independence

The First Continental Congress in Philadelphia did not foresee the issuance of a declaration of independence. The representatives from the 13 colonies and Canada were assembled to air complaints about Britain's alleged abuses of powers in the New World—not to declare independence. But by September of 1774 when the delegates of that First Continental Congress drew up the Declaration of Rights and Grievances to define for King George III the liberties and duties of colonists as they saw them, it was apparent the differences were irreconcilable. The sovereign and British Parliamentary decisions that led to that first convention and the king's subsequent unwillingness to recognize the complaints of the representatives led finally to armed confrontation and the Second Continental Congress, which met in 1776 and drafted the Declaration of Independence.

Broadly speaking, colonists believed internal affairs, such as the levying of taxes and the passing of local laws, to be the rightful jurisdiction of colonial legislatures. However, King George III felt he had the right to raise money from American residents to compensate for the expenses incurred during the French and Indian War and to play an active role in governing his evermore prosperous property—the New World. This difference of opinion between the king and his subjects in America accounted for the eventual decision of the colonists to renounce his authority over them. The Stamp Act, the Townshend Acts, and the Intolerable Acts were all unjust taxes in the eyes of the colonists who were not even allowed representation in Parliament; and King George's restrictions on trade, his dissolving of state legislatures, and his appointing of excessive officers in the colonies were all seen as oppressive measures to a colonial population that had been basically left alone for decades.

Arguably, the king's definition of colonial duties and liberties differed so greatly from the definition offered by the colonists because America was growing up. Originally dependent on Great Britain for money, materials, and new settlers to clear and build in the vast wilderness, the American colonies were—by the second half of the eighteenth century—established and successful farm communities capable of directing their own affairs. Demands by the Crown and the British Parliament that once seemed reasonable and necessary now became intrusive and arrogant. The Declaration of Independence grew naturally out of the time, place, and events that fostered it.

Proud of its heritage and considerable success since revolutionary times, the United States today would like to extend the democratic principles established in the Declaration of Independence to all of the nations of the world. But does democracy make sense in countries lacking the historic, economic, social, and geographic context to support it? In this lesson students read the comments of a fictitious exiled dictator who suggests that conditions must be ripe in a nation— as they were in eighteenth-century America—for democracy to be successful. The student activities that follow allow students to voice their own opinions based on the reading, examine the steps that led to the signing of the Declaration of Independence, see the situation from King George III's point of view, and research less familiar facts about the Declaration of Independence, the American Revolution, and the people and events of the day by engaging in an American Revolution trivia treasure hunt.

Teaching Activities

Freeing the World

Students decide for themselves whether democracy is the best system of government for all of the peoples of the world by answering questions based on the student reading.

Building Tensions

Allow students to choose a partner for this activity. Then copy the Building Tensions pages and distribute a copy to each pair of students who will create flashcards to assist them in examining the sequence of events that led to the signing of the Declaration of Independence and the fighting of the American Revolution.

A Royal Response

Students read passages from the Declaration of Independence and respond to the complaints expressed there from the point of view of the British Crown.

Revolutionary Pursuit

Students have fun learning facts about the events and people surrounding the American Revolution and the drafting of the Declaration of Independence while playing the game of Revolutionary Pursuit. Provide each student with a copy of this page and conduct the activity as a treasure hunt.

1. Have students discuss the courage needed to affix one's name to the Declaration of Independence and write a one-page account of courage they have seen or heard of.

2. Research countries that in modern times have struggled for their independence. What factors do political analysts and historians suggest were involved in the success or failure of their attempts at democracy?

3. Conduct a mock Second Continental Congress in which students represent those present at the original congress and follow parliamentary procedures faithfully.

4. Assign individual or partner reports on the fascinating lives of the 51 signers of the Declaration of Independence.

5. Require each student to research American Revolution books, movies, and Internet sites for ten fascinating, little-known facts to add to the Revolutionary Pursuit game.

INTERVIEW WITH A DICTATOR

General Irin, exiled ruler of an unidentified country, responds to a reporter's question: "Do you believe that democracy is good for your people?"

Why democracy? My name is General Irin, and I live in exile because the great United States decided my people deserved free elections. Until two years ago, life in my country was simple. No one starved, and my army arrested and imprisoned any persons who acted violently. Crime was low and streets were clean. Only one newspaper and a few rebels in the hills cared about voting. Then the American press began circulating terrible rumors about human rights violations under my regime, and suddenly those few rebels in the hills had better weapons supplied by the U.S. government. After inciting this civil insurrection themselves, American forces landed to bring my people peace and democracy.

For a year I have lived in exile with my family. Is there peace now in my country? Is there democracy? No, instead there are political assassinations and car bombings. Crime rules the streets in spite of the American soldiers at every corner, only a fourth of the people bother to vote, and the government—with its "freely elected" officials—has dozens of bickering parties who cannot even agree on a coalition president. The streets are dirty, babies are fed by Red Cross volunteers, and massacres of one ethnic group by another occur regularly. So I ask you, why democracy?

Americans speak fondly and with pride of their own Declaration of Independence and the brave soldiers of the American Revolution. They want to assist the entire world in rising against tyranny and founding representative republics. They station troops in South Korea and Somalia and Bosnia and Haiti and Panama and the Philippines. They invade scores of countries the world over and attempt to set up "little Americas."

But democracy does not work everywhere. To launch a free, representative republic, conditions must be ripe. First, a country needs a common identity that transcends the petty regional, ethnic, and religious differences of its subgroups. Second, it must claim a broad and successful middle class with the education, time, and interest required to vote. Third, a country needs a strong body of common law which they want their government to enforce. Fourth, a country aspiring to democracy needs the economic infrastructure on which it must operate—the schools, roads, farms, factories, bridges, and communication systems that link its communities together.

The 13 American colonies in 1776 had all of this and something more: a common enemy (King George and his Parliament) that stood in the way of economic progress. My country has none of these things. That is why democracy is failing there, bringing ruin and misery to a people who were at least safe and fed under my allegedly brutal military dictatorship.

And my country does not suffer alone. Not having the economic stability in 1992 to sustain a republic, Algeria's first elections were followed by violence, and their second elections were cancelled. Yugoslavian bids for independence brought bloodbaths. Countries in West Africa are democracies by name and chaos by action. In Mexico, 90% of the crimes go unpunished, provincial villagers are slaughtered by men in uniform, and nothing in government works unless bribes are made. In Russia, pensioners starve as industry slowly grinds to a halt and soldiers guarding nuclear weapons go unpaid month after month.

Are these tragedies the purpose of democracy? No, but forcing independence on unwilling, uninterested, and unprepared citizens of still developing nations can only bring instability. Even Jefferson, in your country's famous Declaration of Independence, said, "Prudence, indeed, will dictate that Governments long established should not be changed for light and transient Causes." It was not until "in the course of human events, it became necessary . . ." that America fought its revolution. I urge you to allow my country the same slow, evolutionary steps before you throw a system at us that is destined to bring our unprepared nation only grief and suffering.

On your own paper, answer in complete sentences the following questions, which are based on the student reading.

1. General Irin suggests that democracy is not the best form of government for every nation and that one cannot disregard historic, economic, and social conditions. How does he argue this point?

2. Conversely, it could be argued that all governments should derive their authority from the governed and that any nation that is under the rule of a tyrant deserves a move toward democracy regardless of the nation's historical or current economic, educational, and societal circumstances. With which view do you agree?

3. Why might there be quotation marks around the words "freely elected" in the middle of the second paragraph of General Irin's speech?

4. The United States becomes involved in civil wars and revolutionary struggles in some countries while virtually ignoring the disputes in other lands. How do you think foreign affairs officials make decisions about which rebels to aid in their fights for democracy? Consider geopolitical significance and economic importance.

5. Would you ever live in a nation that was not democratic? Would you live in China if your employer offered you a great deal of money to manage operations of a corporation that had offices in that country? If you lived in a Communist country, what differences would you notice in your everyday life? What if you lived in a country ruled by a military leader or a political tyrant?

6. Alexis de Tocqueville, author of *Democracy in America*, believed that majority rule could be as oppressive as the rule of a despot. What might he have meant by that?

Building Tensions

Cut along the solid lines below to create flashcards. Then with a partner, study the flashcards to learn about the steps that led to the signing of the Declaration of Independence. When each of you has mastered a card, cut it along the solid lines, fold it along the dotted lines, and tape the ends together to create a cube. These are the "building blocks" that led to the construction of the Declaration of Independence. How many blocks can you stack before your tower crumbles? The patriots' tower of complaints soon tumbled into war with Great Britain.

These acts were passed by British Parliament during the seventeenth and eighteenth centuries to protect English trade and industries. Provisions included the requirement that American goods be shipped on boats constructed in England and run with a 75% English crew; tobacco, rice, and indigo could only be exported to England or English colonies; and the manufacturing of some products was restricted to England only and not allowed in any colonies. These acts were not disputed by colonists until heavier taxes were levied under their provisions to pay for the French and Indian wars.

These wars were fought in the Americas between Britain and France. British officials complained that colonists did not cooperate in providing men and supplies and that they continued to trade with the enemy. King George III decided to tax the now prosperous colonists for war expenses and to play a more active role in their governing. Changes came too many and too fast for the colonists who had been virtually left alone for decades.

Americans who believed that they should only be taxed if their own elected representatives voted for such measures were not happy with the slew of revenue-raising policies that Parliament began to pass in 1763. The Sugar Act imposed a duty on imported molasses, the Stamp Act demanded all legal documents be printed on paper with the official British seal, the Quartering Act required colonists to provide troops with housing and provisions, and the Townshend Acts taxed everything from tea to paper to glass.

In addition to the Townshend Acts, Exchequer Charles Townshend also convinced Parliament to establish the American Board of Customs Commissioners to enforce strictly the Navigation Acts. The fact that the Commissioners extorted money from colonists and seized their ships at sea did not add to the trust between colonists and the Crown. And when the king dissolved the Massachusetts legislature for sending a letter to the other colonies condemning the Townshend Acts, tensions rose all the more.

Navigation Acts

French and Indian wars

Taxation Without Representation

Troubles with Townshend

Hostility between colonists and British officials prompted England to station British troops in the Americas. On March 5, 1770, British soldiers fired into a crowd that was taunting them, killing five men. The incident ignited anti-British sentiment in the Americas.

All of the provisions of the Townshend Acts (with the exception of the taxation of tea) were repealed when Americans boycotted British goods. The tea tax and a new Tea Act of 1773 designed to cut the middleman out of selling tea to the Americas for a company called the British East India Company prompted Patriots to destroy 340 chests of tea by throwing them into the harbor at this "party."

These acts, which were issued as punishment for the Boston Tea Party participants, closed the port of Boston, allowed royal officials to be tried in England, and provided for the quartering of troops again. With the passage of these acts, the colonists rallied together in defense of Massachusetts.

This meeting of representatives from the 13 colonies and Canada took place in Philadelphia in September of 1774. The delegates discussed what they considered abuses of the Crown in the Americas and drafted the Declaration of Rights and Grievances.

When British troops learned that Americans were training minutemen in preparation for possible military conflicts with England, they attempted to seize munitions in Massachusetts. On April 19, 1775, fighting broke out in these two towns when Paul Revere and others warned American militia men of the British plan. The American Revolution was underway.

On May 10, 1775, delegates met at this conference to appoint a commander in chief of the Continental Army. Americans were still rebellious colonists at this point, hoping for reconciliation with Britain. When the Olive Branch Petition that affirmed American loyalty to the crown but demanded an end to certain policies was not accepted by the king, this gathering of men drafted the Declaration of Independence establishing American troops not as rebellious British citizens, but as citizens of a new country.

Boston Massacre

Boston Tea Party

Intolerable Acts

First Continental Congress

Lexington and Concord

Second Continental Congress

A Royal Response

American Patriots and the Crown had different ideas of what it meant to be a colonist in the 1700s. If you were King George III and you had just read these complaints taken directly from the Declaration of Independence, how would you respond?

1. "He has forbidden his Governors to pass Laws of immediate and pressing Importance, unless suspended in their Operation till his Assent should be obtained; and when so suspended, he has utterly neglected to attend to them."

   King's Response:

2. "He has dissolved Representative Houses repeatedly, for opposing with manly Firmness his Invasion on the Rights of the People."

   King's Response:

3. "He has erected a Multitude of new Offices, and sent hither Swarms of Officers to harass our People, and eat our Substance."

   King's Response:

4. "He has kept among us, in Times of Peace, Standing Armies, without the consent of our Legislature."

   King's Response:

5. "For cutting off our Trade with all Parts of the World"

   King's Response:

6. "For imposing Taxes on us without our Consent"

   King's Response:

7. "For taking away our Charters, abolishing our most valuable Laws, and altering fundamentally the Forms of our Government"

   King's Response:

8. "Our repeated Petitions have been answered only by repeated Injury."

   King's Response:

Revolutionary Pursuit

Use the Internet, encyclopedias, your history books, and school library books about the American Revolution to locate the answers to the questions below. The first person to complete this page correctly wins Revolutionary Pursuit.

1. At the time of the American Revolution, what percentage of the white population opposed a break with Great Britain?

2. How many of the men who signed the Declaration of Independence were farmers by trade?

3. Following the signing of the Treaty of Paris that ended the American Revolution, George Washington resigned his position as commander in chief of the Continental Army with what words?

4. What brilliant officer who eventually reached the position of major general provided courageous leadership at Ticonderoga alongside Ethan Allen and at Saratoga alongside Horatio Gates, but later died a depressed, unappreciated man in London, England?

5. What word in the Declaration of Independence was probably a misprint in the final copy?

6. Which came first, the signing of the Declaration of Independence or the beginning of the American Revolution?

7. What did Thomas Jefferson think of the changes Congress made to the draft of the Declaration of Independence that he and his committee members wrote?

8. Did George Washington ever fight on the side of the British?

9. How many people fought on the side of the Patriots?

10. On what date was the actual act of independence adopted?

11. Where can you find the original copy of the Declaration of Independence today?

12. Was the Declaration of Independence signed by all delegates at the Continental Congress on July 4, 1776?

13. Who was the last surviving signer of the Declaration of Independence?

14. How many signers of the Declaration of Independence went on to become U.S. presidents?

The United States Constitution

From 1781 through 1788, U.S. citizens were governed by the Articles of Confederation, a document lacking in central authority that created only a loose confederation of the 13 original states. Because it was powerless to levy taxes, regulate trade, or enforce laws, the document proved incapable of governing the new nation. On May 25, 1787, in Philadelphia 55 representatives from 12 of the 13 new states met to attend what was later called the Constitutional Convention to revise the failing Articles of Confederation. The revision process soon gave way to the writing of an entirely new document, and the United States Constitution was born.

The United States Constitution prompted controversy at the time of its drafting. Rhode Island, happy with its state autonomy and lucrative trade industry, refused to even send delegates to the convention and later had to be threatened with foreign nation status and imposition of trade duties before it would ratify the new Constitution. Patrick Henry and Samuel Adams, both signers of the Declaration of Independence, were also absent from the convention, disfavoring the creation of a strong central government. A handful of delegates who did attend the convention believed they had the authority only to revise the Articles of Confederation and withdrew from the proceedings for a time before joining in the drafting of a new document. Conflicts about the composition of the legislative body and the issues surrounding trade almost came to impasses. On September 17, 1787, after 16 weeks of ironing out compromises, only 39 delegates actually signed the resulting document, and the ratification process proved a bitter fight due to the opposition of small farmers and artisans who objected to a strong central government and feared that fundamental individual rights would be squelched under the new Constitution.

A lively and spirited document, the United States Constitution continues to initiate debate today in classrooms, courtrooms, and on Senate floors. Contemporary political ideologies, new research and inventions, and unanticipated social issues demand that the Constitution be reexamined continually as revisions try to keep up with an ever-changing world. The Constitution's broad clauses were constructed to handle future change, and it is the duty of U.S. citizens to see to it that they do.

In this lesson, students read a museum placard that might accompany the United States Constitution as displayed in the National Archives Building in Washington, D.C., to learn how the nation has witnessed so much change over the past two centuries while relying on the same supreme document. Activities and extension ideas focus on weaknesses inherent in the Articles of Confederation, the philosophers whose ideas inspired the Constitution's framers, and the civic responsibilities of modern-day U.S. citizens.

Teaching Activities

Making a Change
Students review the student reading based on the questions in this exercise.

Framing the Framers
Students learn interesting biographical information about the Constitution's ardent supporters and fervent opponents with this matching exercise.

What Went Wrong?
Students learn why the Articles of Confederation was not a viable document from which to form a new nation as they consider problems with no solutions provided in the context of the Articles.

A Puzzling Document
Students examine various aspects of the Constitution, its drafters, and its historical basis as they complete this crossword puzzle.

1. Clip and display newspaper articles which cover issues that continue to inspire Constitutional debates today.

2. Study the writings of both the federalists and the anti-federalists and lead a class debate about the pros and cons of a strong central government.

3. This country's Founding Fathers created a great nation by formulating a constitution and government based on individual citizen participation. Induct your students into civil service in one or more of the following ways:
   a. supervise litter pickup, flower planting, and/or mural painting around your school
   b. write class letters to the president of the United States addressing federal issues that affect minors
   c. invite city, county, and district politicians to speak to your students
   d. join local civic groups (garden clubs, historical societies) in one of their upcoming community projects
   e. arrange for your class to provide monthly artwork to decorate your community's public buildings

4. Research the Internet, libraries, and CD-ROM encyclopedias for information on Locke, Voltaire, Rousseau, and Montesquieu—philosophers who inspired the Founding Fathers.

5. Study the interesting court cases that have modified the interpretation of the Constitution from time to time as well as the history of the document itself and other facts about the Constitution by looking up the exciting Internet site entitled A Road Map to the U.S. Constitution located at http://library.advanced.org/11572/

6. Write to the Center for Civic Education to learn about the annual, national "We the People" Contest, 5146 Douglas Fir Rd., Calabasas, CA 91302 (818) 291-9321.

7. Research and report on the lives of Constitutional Convention delegates.

THE UNITED STATES CONSTITUTION

Imagine that you stand inside the National Archives Building in Washington, D.C., staring at the original United States Constitution. You have just read the first accompanying placard, highlighting the history behind the document. You now turn your attention to Placard II which explains how an old, stable document can allow for the necessary changes in politics and culture that come along with the advancing of time. Read the placard below and answer the questions that follow in the Making a Change activity.

The United States Constitution
Placard II: A Living Document

Although the United States Constitution has remained the supreme law of the land in this country for over 200 years, it is a living document constructed to allow for continual political growth and cultural change. Unlike many other Constitutions, ours is not a compilation of laws, acts, and customs but rather a written set of rules broadly defining the powers and limits of the three branches of government and the rights of citizens and states. Specific local, state, and federal laws do not become a part of the Constitution. Therefore, policy and law changes are relatively easy to achieve in America, provided the changes do not contradict the "Supreme Law of the Land." The Constitution provides for necessary, periodic changes in three main ways.

The Elastic Clause
Article I, Section 8, of the Constitution gives Congress the power "to make laws which shall be necessary and proper for the carrying into Execution the foregoing Powers, and all other Powers vested by the Constitution . . ." This so-called "elastic clause" has been stretched to fit many situations throughout the history of the nation, beginning with the establishment of a federal bank in the early 1800s and continuing today with the passage of bills that regulate everything from business practices to environmental policies.

Judicial Review

Since the 1803 case of *Marbury* v. *Madison*, the courts have claimed the power to determine the constitutionality of laws. This power of Judicial Review has allowed Supreme Court justices to influence policy and law changes throughout America's history. The court's changing views on racial issues proves the point.

The *Dred Scott* v. *Sanford* (1857) case proclaimed that the Constitution did not view blacks as citizens of the United States. An 1883 decision again invalidated black rights by declaring that an eight-year-old Civil Rights Act was unconstitutional. Just over a decade later, a Supreme Court decision upheld segregation, only to reverse its stand in the 1954 *Brown* v. *Board of Education* case. The 1964 Civil Rights Act that banned discrimination on the grounds of "race, color, religion, or national origin" has been upheld by numerous lower and higher courts since its enactment. And the courts continue to modify the interpretation of the Constitution today, influencing laws and policies pertaining to minority rights—and a wide range of other issues.

Voice of the People

Individual citizens influence political policies under the Constitution as well. Citizens are represented in Washington by senators, congresspeople, and the president. They elect state and local representatives too. Citizens vote on local ordinances and state initiatives. They participate in political rallies and state conventions that propose changes in everything from minor stands of their party to new amendments to the Constitution. Citizens write, call, and visit public officials and hire professional lobbying groups to promote their interests in Congress. Everyone has a say in a democracy. The Constitution is flexible enough to bend with the times. In America the people are not in service to the Constitution—the Constitution is in service to the people.

Making a Change

On your own sheet of paper, answer in complete sentences the following questions, which are based on the student reading.

1. The student reading mentions professional lobbying groups as a means of influencing changes in laws and public policies. What do you see as the pros and cons of the presence of lobbying groups in America?

2. In 1803 Chief Justice John Marshall declared an act of congress unconstitutional and set the precedent for Judicial Review—a power not directly given the courts by the Constitution. Are Supreme Court justices overstepping their intended duties when they assume the powers of Judicial Review?

3. As mentioned in the student reading, the United States Constitution is not a documentation of laws but rather a framework that defines the relationship among the three branches of government. What are some of the checks and balances built into the Constitution that prevent one branch from gaining too much power?

4. Several states ratified the Constitution on the condition that it include a Bill of Rights. What fundamental rights might have been endangered if our Constitution did not include the first ten amendments?

5. The United States Constitution has only been amended 27 times in over two centuries. What kinds of changes have the amendments instituted? How is an amendment added to the Constitution? Why do you think the amendment process is rather complicated?

6. Although the Constitution allows for changes in laws and policies, some parts of the document itself are no longer in effect due to the passage of time or to the addition of an amendment. Find at least five examples of inactive phrases in the Constitution.

Framing the Framers

The frames below contain biographies—instead of portraits—of some of the signers of the Constitution. In a history book or encyclopedia, locate information about the patriots named in the middle of the page to help you match the names of the Constitution signers with their biographies.

Frame One

At the age of 27, this New Jersey delegate became the youngest signer of the Constitution. In later years, he was indicted for treason when he supported Aaron Burr's attempt to create an empire in the South.

Frame Two

This Virginia delegate to the Constitutional Convention did not take the floor once or serve on any committees, but attended all sessions and worked for the ratification of the resulting document.

Frame Three

This "Father of the Constitution" and later congressman, secretary of state, and president of the nation, took the floor at the convention 150 times, served on numerous committees, provided the most complete journal of events, and coauthored *The Federalist Papers* to encourage ratification of the Constitution. A slave owner himself, he—in later years—worked with a group who wished to resettle slaves in Africa.

Frame Four

One of the most capable speakers at the convention, this two-time candidate for president enjoyed a lifelong career in politics. As an outspoken opponent of slavery, he believed a system of compensation for slave owners was necessary in putting an end to the practice.

Frame Five

This aide-de-camp to George Washington during the American Revolution, coauthor of *The Federalist Papers*, and creator of the nation's first bank who believed only the wealthy, educated elite were suited to govern the nation, was killed in a duel with a political rival, Aaron Burr.

Frame Six

This kite-flying scientist and printer who claimed 12 siblings attended less than two years of school. He invented bifocals; proved lightning was a form of electricity; wrote annual editions of the best selling *Poor Richard's Almanac;* established schools, libraries, and hospitals; and served as a great and patriotic negotiator who encouraged French support of the American Revolution, ironed out the terms of the Treaty of Paris, and promoted the compromises that resulted in the writing and ratification of the United States Constitution.

Alexander Hamilton

Jonathan Dayton

James Madison

Rufus King

Benjamin Franklin

John Blair

Framing the Framers (Cont'd.)

Numerous American patriots did not sign the Constitution. Some were absent from the Convention on the day of the signing, some did not support the final form of the document, and others refused even to attend the convention because it supported a strong central government. Locate information about the men named in the middle of the page in your history book or an encyclopedia and match their names to their biographies.

Frame Seven

This American patriot who, in 1775, demanded war with Great Britain yelling, "Give me liberty or give me death," did not attend the convention or support the ratification of the Constitution because he feared it would trample state and individual rights.

Frame Eight

Primary author of the Declaration of Independence and later president of the nation, this admired statesman did not attend the convention or sign the Constitution because he was out of the country in 1787 serving as the United States minister to France.

Oliver Ellsworth

Thomas Jefferson

John Hancock

Elbridge Gerry

Luther Martin

Patrick Henry

Frame Nine

This pompous and unpopular convention delegate is said to have "objected to everything he did not propose." Although he walked out of the proceedings and did not sign the Constitution, he supported the document following its ratification and became active in state politics. When he redefined his district in the shape of a salamander to ensure its power in the Senate, he promoted the coining of the term "gerrymander."

Frame Ten

This Maryland delegate walked out of the Convention after protesting the secrecy of the Constitution's drafting, the absence of a Supreme Court jury, and what he believed to be the placing of individual and state concerns above the needs of the new nation by some delegates.

Frame Eleven

This signer of the Declaration of Independence distrusted a strong central government and did not attend the convention but supported the Constitution's ratification when he presided over his state's convention.

Frame Twelve

This Connecticut delegate played an active role in the convention, serving on the committee that prepared the first draft of the Constitution and suggesting the term "United States" be used instead of "national" when referring to the country in the document. However, he was in his own state on business on September 17, 1787, and so not present at the convention on that day to sign the Constitution.

What Went Wrong?

In 1776 John Dickinson prepared the original draft of the Articles of Confederation—the United States' first constitution. As written the Articles provided for a strong national government, but the new Americans feared central authority. Therefore, a substantially revised document was ratified in 1781. The ratified Articles established only a loose confederation of states with a very limited federal government. Consider the weaknesses of America's first constitution in the left-hand column and write an example of a situation that would find no remedy in the document. An example has been done for you.

WEAKNESS	SITUATION WITH NO RESOLVE
1. Congress had no power to tax. It could only request funds from states that often refused its requests.	1. The federal government could not pay off its Revolutionary War debts. 2. The federal government did not have the money to maintain an army.
2. A federal court system was not established.	
3. Congress had no power to regulate trade.	
4. State governments could print money along with the federal government.	
5. States were not prohibited from entering into agreements with other nations.	
6. Amendments to the Articles of Confederation required ratification by all 13 state legislatures.	

A Puzzling Document

Get out your history book, open your classroom encyclopedias, research your school library, quiz your friends, and get online in an attempt to complete this crossword puzzle and add to your knowledge of the origins and details of the United States Constitution.

ACROSS

1. a philosopher who believed the government must promote the general welfare, even at the expense of some individual rights

4. number of original states in the Union

6. The United States' first constitution was the _____ of Confederation.

9. citizens who did not wish to ratify the Constitution because it gave too much power to Congress and the executive branch and did not contain a bill of rights

11. the branch of the legislature that contains two representatives from each state

12. the number of the amendment that provides the freedoms of speech, press, religion, and assembly

13. a philosopher whose definition of the ideal state as outlined in his work, *The Republic*, greatly influenced the Founding Fathers

14. Only 27 of these changes to the Constitution have been added in the past two centuries.

15. oldest delegate at the convention (two words)

17. the Supreme Court case that established the powers of Judicial Review

DOWN

2. number of years the United States citizens lived under the Articles of Confederation

3. commander in chief of the United States Army

5. The court's authority to determine the constitutionality of laws is called Judicial _____.

7. president of the Constitutional Convention

8. a plan drafted by James Madison that proposed a two-house legislature with representation proportional to state size (two words)

10. ninth state to ratify the Constitution, thereby putting it into effect (two words)

16. the philosopher who first suggested that life, liberty, and property were fundamental rights

The Bill of Rights

The first ten amendments to the United States Constitution are called the Bill of Rights because they codify the protection of individual rights. The amendments were drafted by James Madison during the first meeting of the United States Congress in March of 1789 to "extend the ground of public confidence in the government." Many citizens expressed concern that the newly ratified Constitution lacked a guarantee of individual freedoms. Six states submitted proposed amendments along with their ratification statements; and New York, Virginia, Massachusetts, and Pennsylvania refused to ratify the Constitution at all without the assurance that a Bill of Rights would amend the document.

James Madison did not start from scratch in drafting the Bill of Rights. The amendments referring to the prohibition of excessive bail and cruel and unusual punishment are direct descendants of the English Bill of Rights. The Virginia Declaration of Rights served as another model for Madison. And 103 amendments were submitted to the Congress by the individual states as well as 42 more proposed by minority groups within the states.

Madison's resulting proposal to Congress compressed the numerous recommendations into 16 amendments which he suggested be included in the body of the Constitution. Congressional debates resulted in paring down the amendments even further to 12 and determining that they take the form of individual amendments to be tacked on to the end of the Constitution. The states ratified 10 of the 12 amendments, refusing to validate two having to do with congressional size and compensation.

The main purposes of the Bill of Rights are to protect the minority from the majority and to limit the powers and prevent abuses by the legislative and executive branches. Unlike many other statements of freedoms including the French Declaration of the Rights of Man and of the Citizen—also adopted in 1789—the United States Bill of Rights is not a statement of principle alone, but is enforceable by the courts.

Today the Bill of Rights remains an important document both for the American people who continue to refer to it in issues involving the freedom of speech, the press, religion, and more—but also for peoples of the world who consider it a standard example of a document protecting basic human rights.

In this activity students debate current First Amendment issues presented in the student readings and examine the entire Bill of Rights through student activities. Extension ideas suggest students create a minor's version of the Bill of Rights and direct students to further information on all of the Constitution's amendments and current individual freedoms issues.

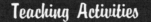

Teaching Activities

Student Readings: Freedom of Speech, the Press, and Religion

Divide your class into three groups and assign one group the reading of Student Reading A, another the reading of Student Reading B, and the final group the reading of Student Reading C. Require each group to complete the questions that accompany its reading. Then allow each group to present views and information from both sides of the debate about which they have read and answered questions. Students may choose to present information in the form of a debate, an oral report, the presentation of charts, graphs, and visuals, or some combination thereof.

I Know My Rights

Students examine the Bill of Rights and pertinent current issues.

The Standard in Human Rights

Students compare and contrast the Bill of Rights with the United Nation's Universal Declaration of Human Rights and Canada's Charter of Rights and Freedoms.

1. Children must learn a great deal before they can exercise freedoms wisely. Parents may demand that children wear seat belts, eat their vegetables, or brush their teeth. But there are some rights even children should have. A child deserves to be fed, clothed, and bathed. Compose a Bill of Rights outlining the rights and freedoms every child deserves. Are there children in the world (or even in our own country) who do not enjoy these basic fundamental freedoms?

2. Study the history and specifics of Amendments 11 through 27. Draw a time line or create a game to help yourself and others in memorizing the amendments to the United States Constitution.

3. At various times throughout the history of our country, individuals and groups of citizens have pushed for the addition of amendments to the Constitution. Some people today argue that the Constitution should include an amendment stating that infants born in the United States of illegal alien parents should not be considered citizens of the United States. Others today are pushing for the reconsideration of an amendment to allow prayers in school (an amendment that failed ratification in 1984). Do you support these amendment recommendations? Why or why not?

4. Clip and post newspaper articles that address Bill of Rights issues. Have students identify the amendment to which the article refers.

5. Research countries that prohibit free speech or the practice of certain religions. What have individuals endured in the past for speaking against governments or practicing unpopular religions? What do they endure today?

6. Demonstrate the religious diversity of the world by labeling a world map according to the major and minor religions of each region.

FREEDOM OF SPEECH

In 1918, near the end of World War I, Eugene Victor Debs—two time candidate for president and then leader of America's Socialist Party—found himself in jail. In June of that year, he had remarked in a speech before the Ohio State Socialist Convention that World War I was not a war of principle, but of capitalistic greed. He had criticized President Wilson and the very acts under which he would be convicted: the Espionage and Sedition Acts of 1917 and 1918 which outlawed not only treasonous activity, but even any words that might dampen the morale of American soldiers or be considered a criticism of the U.S. government, Constitution, or flag. Although enforced only during the war years, 1,500 individuals were brought to trial under these acts which were upheld by the courts as constitutional with the argument that curtailing the First Amendment right to the freedom of speech was necessary during times of war when the words spoken established a "clear and present danger."

The freedom to speak without the fear of government restraint is taken for granted by Americans today, but it is not common to all people of the world. In fact, only the United States, Japan, English-speaking countries, and the democracies of Western Europe have codified protections for those who voice unpopular opinions and beliefs. Yet even these countries are not completely free from censorship. In the United States, laws have been made and upheld by the courts that prohibit speech that threatens national security or civil order, is slanderous, or is obscene. During the Civil War period, the southern states outlawed all written statements against slavery. A New York lawsuit in 1925 determined that words advocating the forceful overthrow of the government could be prohibited. In more recent years, producers of music, television programs, radio programs, and movies have censored their own works by developing ratings systems and banning certain words from use on the airwaves to avoid court cases and prevent public disdain. Communities exert pressure on school librarians and textbook publishers to include and exclude various ideas and information, and the courts continue to modify the interpretation of the First Amendment's assertion that "Congress shall make no law . . . abridging the freedom of speech."

Based on the student reading and the opinions of those in your group, answer the following questions about the limits on the freedom of speech. Then formulate a presentation of your ideas either using speeches, role-playing dramas, a computer, video, overhead projector display, or other means of conveying information.

1. Do you believe the Founding Fathers intended there to be any limits on the freedom of speech in America?

2. Does it make sense to limit speech that could cause an overthrow of the government or civil unrest or an unsafe situation for soldiers during times of war?

3. Do you think it is Constitutional to outlaw obscene language?

4. What restrictions does your school put on student and staff language? Does your school have rules against foul language? Put-downs of other students? "Fighting" words? Deliberate lies? Do these rules make sense?

5. Justice Oliver Wendell Holmes, presenting a Supreme Court finding in the late 1900s, said that if words would create a "clear and present danger," they could not legally be uttered. He gave the example of how a man yelling "Fire!" in a theater when no fire existed would cause panic and perhaps injury to the theater patrons. Does the "clear and present danger" standard seem just in deciding when free speech can be restricted?

6. Are symbolic acts, such as flag burning and the wearing of armbands in protest of a war, covered under the First Amendment's protection of free speech?

7. In writing the First Amendment, the Founding Fathers were protecting the rights of those who had unpopular opinions and beliefs. In 1978 American Nazis—individuals considered by many as enemies of free speech—wished to hold a rally in a predominantly Jewish neighborhood. They were told they could not do so by the town leaders. The courts disagreed and ruled that the city could not limit public demonstrations. Do you agree with the town's or the court's decision? Why?

8. Would completely unrestricted speech create social chaos?

FREEDOM OF THE PRESS

In 1735 John Peter Zenger was acquitted of libel when his newspaper published articles criticizing the policies of New York's colonial governor because the published articles were true. This "truth test" in libel suits was until then unheard of. In Europe at the time, anything said against the government was considered seditious and was punishable as such.

In the United States the press is free to print material without post or prior government review. Yet as with the freedom of speech, the extent to which the press is free is determined by the courts on a case-by-case basis. Libelous written statements are illegal, but public officials (including some celebrities) can only expect to collect damages if they can prove the author of the remarks either knew they were untrue or did not even attempt to determine their truth. Some classified materials are not available to the public due to national security concerns, although this type of censorship was greatly reduced with the Pentagon Papers decision in which Nixon's administration was informed it could not stop the publication of a document that revealed government lies about Vietnam. However, as recently as Grenada in 1983 and the Gulf War in 1991, the press has been barred from covering at least the initial ground war stages of modern-day conflicts. Likewise the press has been prohibited from releasing certain police records or covering some legal cases in the interest of justice. The Freedom of Information Act (1966) and the Privacy Act (1974) allow individual citizens to request government records including those pertaining to the citizens themselves, but there still exists no clear-cut line between what can (or even must) be published and what printed words will not be allowed.

Today's biggest freedom of the press controversy is playing itself out on the Internet—a terrain some claim cannot by nature conform to rules and restrictions. Others demand that software be highly regulated to include safeguards, for example, limiting access by minors. The question remains— where does one man's freedom infringe on another man's equally protected rights? For the most part, if it is not obscene or pornographic, if it does not threaten national security or promote the active, violent overthrow of the government, and if it is not a lie, it can be published in the United States.

After your group has finished reading Student Reading B, answer the following questions and then prepare a presentation on the freedoms and limitations of the press in the United States. Make your presentation creative, using speeches, role-playing, visualization, computer or video images, or any other means you may think of to convey your information.

1. In Great Britain the press cannot disclose any government documents without permission nor can it write about any case presently before the court. Is this good policy? Why or why not?

2. Should a person be free to publish a book about anything at all? How about a book with instructions for making a bomb? A book promoting the violent overthrow of the government or the murdering of a specific ethnic group? A book full of known lies about a public official?

3. Should a person be free to write anything including bomb-making instructions or suggestions of illegal actions when writing to a single, specific person such as in a personal letter?

4. Some suggest the Founders only meant for political discourse to be free. They believe allowing obscenity in literature and art carries the freedom of expression far beyond the intent of the First Amendment. What do you think?

5. How does publishing something on the Internet differ from publishing something in a book? Should there be limitations as to what can be said on the Internet? How about in personal e-mail messages that are intended for one specific person?

6. The Internet connects computers around the globe. Should one have to adhere to the laws of the country from which he or she is writing in deciding what can be said online? Should one adhere to the laws of the country to which he or she is sending the message? Should universal laws be constructed to regulate what can be said on the Internet?

7. According to the Fifth Amendment, no person in the United States "shall be compelled in any criminal case to be a witness against himself." Should courts then allow personal diaries as evidence in criminal cases, assuming a warrant was issued?

STUDENT READING C
FREEDOM OF RELIGION

According to the First Amendment, "Congress shall make no law respecting an establishment of religion, or prohibiting the free exercise thereof." In modern times, this has been interpreted to mean there must exist a separation between the church and state. Historically, this separation concept has not existed. The biblical book of Deuteronomy contains what is believed to be the oldest canons on war. Treaties and laws that governed Greek city-states were sanctioned by religious leaders. Roman statues were based on what were believed to be "natural laws" ordained by gods. Popes shared powers with kings for centuries. And England, Scotland, and other countries even today whose citizens do enjoy religious freedom also proclaim an official state religion.

Establishing the separation of church and state concept as the legal standard of religious freedom in America has worked both to simplify and complicate the interpretation of the First Amendment. The concept makes it emphatically illegal to declare a state religion or to establish legal requirements for the qualification of public office (outlawed not only by the First Amendment, but also specifically in Article VI of the Constitution). Yet other issues become all the more confused under the state-religion separation test. Courts decided Mormons could not practice their church-encouraged custom of polygamy in America, but minors can drink the alcohol of Christian communions and Native Americans can use otherwise illegal drugs in religious ceremonies. Prayers and Bible verse readings cannot be mandated by school districts, but religious clubs can meet before and after school hours on school grounds and parents can collect government reimbursement for the bus fare their children must pay to be transported to private religious schools. Nativity scenes cannot be displayed on the steps of state capitol buildings, but federal prisoners can request special foods and unusual items as necessary for the ceremonial practice of their religions.

The line between church and state is a difficult one to draw and citizens from various religious backgrounds contend religion, morals, and ethics necessarily play into legal decisions if laws are to be good ones. Abortion, assisted suicide, the medical use of marijuana, and capital punishment have all proven to be both legal and ethical dilemmas that simply do not make separating religion and the state easy.

Following a reading of Student Reading C, complete the following questions with your group members and prepare a presentation of the rights and limitations afforded Americans in their religious beliefs and practices.

1. There are references to God in our national motto, our pledge of allegiance, and on our money. Does the wording of the First Amendment demand that the state and the church remain separate or just that citizens be free to believe and worship according to their own consciences?

2. Although the authors of the Bill of Rights wished for Puritans, Quakers, and Catholics to be able to worship in their own ways, they did not foresee a nation that would one day be home to Buddhists, Muslims, Christians, and Jews alike. Do you think the church-state separation standard is necessary today because of this diversity? Is there a better "ruler" with which to "measure" whether a practice or law lives up to the intent of the First Amendment to allow citizens religious freedom?

3. How "separate" should schools be from religion? Should they be allowed to call their winter break "Christmas break"? Should they be able to include Christian songs in their "Christmas" program? Should they include a moment of silence at the beginning of each day for students to pray or be silent? Should parents be allowed to pull their students out of classes that teach evolution, sex education, or other facts or theories that conflict with their religious convictions? Should world religions be studied as part of history class?

4. Does the presence of an official religion in a country necessarily restrain the free practice of other religions? Is declaring an official religion a positive or negative policy? Why would it never happen in the United States?

5. Some American citizens are hoping to add a school prayer amendment to the Constitution. Would such an amendment violate the rights of minority religions? Is an amendment necessary for prayer to exist in schools?

The Bill of Rights

Amendment 1: Congress shall make no law respecting an establishment of religion, or prohibiting the free exercise thereof; or abridging the freedom of speech, or of the press; or the right of the people peaceably to assemble, and to petition the government for a redress of grievances.

Amendment 2: A well-regulated militia, being necessary to the security of a free state, the right of the people to keep and bear arms, shall not be infringed.

Amendment 3: No soldier shall, in time of peace be quartered in any house, without the consent of the owner, nor in time of war, but in a manner to be prescribed by law.

Amendment 4: The right of the people to be secure in their persons, houses, papers, and effects, against unreasonable searches and seizures, shall not be violated, and no warrants shall issue, but upon probable cause, supported by oath or affirmation, and particularly describing the place to be searched, and the persons or things to be seized.

Amendment 5: No person shall be held to answer for a capital, or otherwise infamous crime, unless on a presentment or indictment of a grand jury, except in cases arising in the land or naval forces, or in the militia, when in actual service in time of war or public danger; nor shall any person be subject for the same offense to be twice put in jeopardy of life or limb; nor shall be compelled in any criminal case to be a witness against himself, nor be deprived of life, liberty, or property, without due process of law; nor shall private property be taken for public use, without just compensation.

Amendment 6: In all criminal prosecutions, the accused shall enjoy the right to a speedy and public trial, by an impartial jury of the state and district wherein the crime shall have been committed, which district shall have been previously ascertained by law, and to be informed of the nature and cause of the accusation; to be confronted with the witnesses against him; to have compulsory process for obtaining witnesses in his favor, and to have the assistance of counsel for his defense.

Amendment 7: In suits at common law, where the value in controversy shall exceed twenty dollars, the right of a trial by jury shall be preserved, and no fact tried by a jury, shall be otherwise reexamined in any courts of the United States, than according to the rules of the common law.

Amendment 8: Excessive bail shall not be required, nor excessive fines imposed, nor cruel and unusual punishments inflicted.

Amendment 9: The enumeration in the Constitution, of certain rights, shall not be construed to deny or disparage others retained by the people.

Amendment 10: The powers not delegated to the United States by the Constitution, nor prohibited by it to the states, are reserved to the states respectively, or to the people.

I Know My Rights

Read the Bill of Rights in its entirety as presented on the previous page and then complete the following exercises.

I. On your own paper, rewrite the ten amendments that constitute the Bill of Rights using twentieth-century language.

II. Which amendment contained in the Bill of Rights do you believe is the most essential in the modern world? Which is the least important today? On your own paper, defend your position in a one- to three-page persuasive essay.

III. Match the current-day issues below to the amendment to which they pertain.

A. The National Rifleman's Association argues against gun control laws.
Amendment #_____

B. Evidence in a criminal case is thrown out because the police who collected it did not have a warrant.
Amendment #_____

C. An accused defendant requests a defense attorney be provided him by the state.
Amendment #_____

D. Christian fundamentalist groups work to create legislation that would restore prayer in public schools.
Amendment #_____

E. The county pays you for the strip of your front lawn they will distort to widen the street in front of your house.
Amendment #_____

F. The courts debate what can and cannot be said over the Internet.
Amendment #_____

G. The citizens of a given state debate the issue of capital punishment.
Amendment #_____

H. Not being directly addressed in the Constitution, states claim the right to decide for themselves whether to create laws in support of or against assisted suicide for terminally ill patients.
Amendment #_____

I. A group advocating the needs of the homeless argues that just because the Bill of Rights does not specifically mention the right of the people to have adequate food, clothing, and shelter does not mean the people do not have this right.
Amendment #_____

The Standard in Human Rights

The Bill of Rights has served as a model to freedom fighters and authors of human rights documents the world over. Write the letters of the phrases from each column from the Canadian Charter of Rights and Freedoms and the phrases from the Universal Declaration of Human Rights (a United Nations resolution) which are similar in meaning and intent on the blank beside the phrase from the Bill of Rights. The first one has been done for you.

Bill of Rights	*Canadian Charter of*	*Universal Declaration*
Q, L A. Congress shall make no law respecting an establishment of religion.	B. Everyone has the . . . freedom of expression.	C. Everyone has the right to life, liberty, and security of person.
____ D. . . . nor cruel and unusual punishments inflicted	E. Everyone has the . . . freedom of peaceful assembly.	F. Everyone is entitled . . . to a fair and public hearing.
____ G. Congress shall make no law . . . abridging the freedom of speech.	H. Everyone has the right to life, liberty, and the security of person.	I. No one shall be subjected to . . . cruel, inhuman, or degrading . . . punishment.
____ J. . . . nor be deprived of life, liberty, or property	K. . . . the right not to be subjected to any cruel and unusual treatment or punishment	L. . . . the right to freedom of thought, conscience, and religion
____ M. . . . the right to a speedy public trial	N. . . . the right to . . . a trial and public hearing	O. Everyone has the right to freedom of opinion and expression.
____ P. . . . the right of the people peaceably to assemble	Q. Everyone has the . . . freedom of conscience and religion.	R. . . . freedom of peaceful assembly and association
____ S. . . . the right . . . to be secure . . . against unreasonable searches and seizures	T. . . . the right not to be arbitrarily detained	U. . . . the will of the people shall be the basis of authority of government
____ V. The powers not delegated by the Constitution are reserved to the people.	W. the right to be secure against unreasonable search or seizure	X. No one shall be subjected to arbitrary arrest, detention, or exile.
____ Y. No person shall be held unless on . . . indictment . . .	Z. Every citizen of Canada has the right to vote.	AA. No one shall be subjected to arbitrary interference . . . .

The Emancipation Proclamation

The enslaving of human beings dates back to prehistoric times, but the true institutionalization of slavery—wherein individuals are legally considered property, subjected to the will of an "owner," and forced to perform work—did not appear until the rise of early agricultural societies. Chinese, Indian, Egyptian, and Aztec people all enslaved war prisoners, convicted criminals, and indebted citizens to perform tasks in construction, agriculture, and domestic affairs. Ancient Greece condoned slavery as did ancient Rome, although the freeing of slaves was common in both of these empires where freedmen, formerly enslaved for debts or crimes, could move on to socially and politically influential positions later in life.

Spanish, British, and French colonies in North and South America imported slave labor from Africa to develop new lands and build needed infrastructure. Although the first toilers to arrive in Jamestown in 1619 were actually indentured servants, their status had changed to full-fledged slaves by the time of the American Revolution as the expansion of southern plantations made their "free services" almost an economic necessity.

Although slaves maintained a limited number of legal rights including support for the sick and the ability to press certain lawsuits in court, many statesmen and religious groups abhorred the institution of slavery from the very beginnings of our country when such men as Thomas Jefferson, George Washington, and James Madison believed the practice opposed the principles outlined in the Declaration of Independence. Quakers had long argued for the abolition of slavery, the Presbyterian and Methodist Episcopal Churches had spoken against the practice in writings and proclamations, and by 1803 the United States had banned the future importation of slaves from Africa.

Regardless of this abolitionist sentiment, the United States' 1804 census found 3,953,760 enslaved individuals toiling the land and performing domestic duties in the southern states of our nation—and a multitude of free citizens from all regions fighting over whether new territories would be admitted to the Union as free or slave states. In 1854 the Kansas-Nebraska Act, which repealed the long-fought-over Missouri Compromise and allowed the settlers of new territories to decide the question of slavery for themselves, alarmed abolitionists who hoped to at least prevent the spread of slavery, if not to see its immediate elimination. Antislavery groups quickly formed the Republican Party and launched John C. Fremont into the 1856 national campaign for the presidency. Although Fremont lost the election by a narrow margin, the republicans' 1860 candidate who argued that slavery was "a moral, a social, and a political wrong" became the nation's sixteenth president. Abraham Lincoln's election started the series of events that led to the American Civil War, the issuing of the Emancipation Proclamation, and the passage of the Thirteenth Amendment outlawing slavery in any and all states of this nation.

Although the Emancipation Proclamation did not eliminate all slavery on its own accord—and was perhaps as much a political move as an act of justice—the document turned the tide on slavery forever. The Civil War was suddenly being fought to free the slaves, the Thirteenth Amendment gained congressional approval, and the world would never look at slavery the same way again.

In this lesson, students examine the Emancipation Proclamation from its historical context and consider its influence on the slow evolution of civil rights as they imagine viewing a documentary about the document. Student activities and extension ideas focus on American Civil War battles, famous abolitionists, blacks in the army, civil rights action groups and the civil rights movement, and historic Emancipation Proclamation celebrations.

Teaching Activities

Perspectives on the Proclamation
Students answer questions based on the student reading with members of a group.

Slavery to the Tenth Degree
Students rank binding conditions from history and modern times as to their degree of enslavement as they become aware that many restrictive environments exist between complete slavery and true social, economic, and political equality.

I Didn't Know That!
Allow students to check their Civil War IQ as they take this true/false quiz full of little-known facts about the war, slavery, abolitionists, and the Reconstruction period.

And the March Goes On
Students study significant civil rights groups, individuals, and movements that have attempted to make all U.S. citizens equal—legally and actually.

1. Abolitionists in the United States included Quakers, renowned statesmen, and common citizens. Their voices were heard when William Lloyd Garrison began publishing *The Liberator*, a Boston newspaper that demanded an immediate end to slavery. Their sincerity was felt when Harriet Tubman and Levi Coffin took their turns as conductors on the Underground Railroad. Their cause was politically legitimized when the Tappan brothers presented voters with presidential candidates from the Liberty, Free Soil, and later Republican Party who condemned the practice of slavery.

   Research the abolitionist movement in the United States, focusing on the differences between the militant American Anti-Slavery Society, which included such "radicals" as John Brown, who denied the validity of any laws pertaining to slavery, and the American and Foreign Anti-slavery Society, which included such "gradualists" as James Birney and Theodore Weld who promoted legal means of effecting change in slavery policies. Conduct a class debate on the advantages and disadvantages in each approach to ending slavery in this country. Discuss other times in history and in daily life when the radical approach seems appropriate and when the gradual approach will likely be most successful.

2. On January 1, 1863, President Lincoln bid farewell to his guests at a New Year's Day reception at the White House, gathered with a few friends in his study, and signed the Emancipation Proclamation. As telegraph messages reached the large cities declaring that the document had been signed, celebrations broke out everywhere. Blacks and whites shook hands, sang, danced, and threw confetti long into the night in Washington, D.C., New York City, Boston, and beyond. And for the first hundred years afterwards, January first was a busy day of celebration for African-American communities throughout the country as their residents remembered the signing of the Emancipation Proclamation with bands, parades, speeches, and readings of the document in community schools and churches.

   Recapture the excitement in your own classroom by celebrating the signing of the Emancipation Proclamation with a party complete with late nineteenth-century music, early American foods, and red, white, and blue decorations. Assign one student to read the Proclamation and another to address the party with a speech. Speeches of past celebrations sometimes called for equal rights or forgiving attitudes towards former slave owners. What would a speech of today urge citizens to do in the area of race relations?

3. The Thirteenth, Fourteenth, and Fifteenth Amendments are known as the Reconstruction Amendments as they were intended to restore order and rebuild the South following the Civil War. Research and report on the stormy Reconstruction years and the rise and fall of the Republican Party in the South.

4. Research and report on the causes of the Civil War including economic, social, and political factors as well as the compromises, acts, and court cases that brought the slavery issue to the foreground.

5. Assist students in gaining an appreciation for the intensity of a war that pitted brother against brother, dragged on for four years, accrued $5 billion in property damages, and claimed more United States' victims than any other war Americans have participated in by dividing students into groups to research and report on the following:
   A. The Confederacy's war strategy
   B. The Union's war strategy
   C. The effects of geography on the war
   D. The differences in Southern and Northern infrastructure
   E. Civil War weapons
   F. The financial aspects of war
   G. The everyday lives of Confederate and Union soldiers

6. One million, six hundred thousand Union soldiers and 1,000,000 Confederate soldiers including teenage boys, disguised women, and men young and old fought in nearly 2,500 official battles and countless, daily unnamed skirmishes during the American Civil War. Assign groups of students to research and report on the specifics of famous and lesser-known battles of the war. Be certain one group covers Fort Sumter, the first conflict, another the Battle of Antietam—the signal for President Lincoln to make his preliminary proclamation—another the Battle of Gettysburg where Lee lost 25,000 men and Meade lost 23,000, and another the surrender of Lee at Appomattox Court House.

7. Share with your class the exceptional text and pictures that document the contribution of youth in the Civil War in the Scholastic book by Jim Murphy entitled *The Boys' War*.

8. View and report on one of these films based on slavery, forced labor, or servitude: *Kidnapped, Armistad, Tale of Two Cities, Schindler's List, Roots, Ben-Hur, Sophie's Choice, Cool Hand Luke, Bridge on the River Kwai, David Copperfield, Gone with the Wind*, and *Uncle Tom's Cabin*. Most are available in the original novel form as well. Parental discretion may be advised for the film versions.

Emancipation Proclamation:

Historical Perspective, Present-Day Significance

Program Four in the Historical Documents Series

Good evening, and welcome to Program Four in the Historical Documents Series. This evening's documentary focuses on one of the great state documents of the United States—the Emancipation Proclamation. On January 1, 1863, two years into the American Civil War, President Abraham Lincoln proclaimed that "all persons held as slaves within designated states and parts of states, are, and hereforth shall be, free . . ." But what was the historical significance of his proclamation? And what importance does it hold for us today? Let's first place the document in its proper historical context.

HISTORICAL PERSPECTIVE

Abraham Lincoln's entire presidency was plagued by national conflict. A member of the Republican Party, he was known to oppose the concept of slavery. During the Lincoln-Douglas debates, he called it "a moral, a social, and a political wrong." This did not offend the Northerners whose economy was based on trade and whose institutions could embrace the ideals he expressed, but it angered the Southerners considerably. With an economy dependent on slavery and a belief that the Constitution safeguarded the practice, Southern states believed the election of Lincoln would extinguish their way of life and so vowed to leave the Union should he become the nation's sixteenth president. Beginning with South Carolina, 11 states (plus some citizens of Missouri and Kentucky, which officially remained with the Union) seceded from the nation and established the government of the Confederate States of America.

Although opposed to slavery, Lincoln's main purpose in issuing the Emancipation Proclamation was not to free slaves, but to preserve the Union. By July of 1862, the Civil War had been in progress for over a year and a half and the battles were for the most part indecisive. Both sides were losing more men than anticipated, the drafting of soldiers was angering civilians, and everyone was ready to see an end to the conflict. The Emancipation Proclamation would make the abolition of slavery a war aim. This would dissuade France and Great Britain—both of whom had already outlawed slavery—from assisting the Confederates. It would also enable Union officers to disregard fugitive slave laws and use runaway slaves as soldiers. In addition, the proclamation would give the Union army and the Northern public a needed moral boost as their struggle would gain the lofty goal of freeing the slaves.

THE SPECIFICS

Lincoln waited to issue a preliminary proclamation on September 22 on the advice of his cabinet who suggested it should follow in the footsteps of a Union battle victory. So when Lee gave up on an idea to invade the North following heavy losses at the Battle of Antietam, Lincoln declared that in 100 days, all slaves in states deemed in rebellion at the time would be declared free. And on January 1, 1863, Lincoln signed into effect the Emancipation Proclamation.

Only slaves in Confederate states were freed under the order, and those states (or parts of states) under Union control were exempt from the requirements of the proclamation. Border states in which resided men who fought on both sides of the conflict were not affected by the document. Hundreds of thousands of slaves would remain in bondage following the president's words on January 1, 1863.

PRESENT-DAY SIGNIFICANCE

Even so, the Emancipation Proclamation is one of the most significant documents in American history because it reversed an entrenched practice. With the Thirteenth Amendment, remaining slaves throughout the nation joined brothers and sisters freed by the document and the North's victory in the Civil War. Congress established the Freedmen's Bureau to build schools, provide food, and assist in the location of work for newly freed slaves. The Republican Party placed blacks in city, state, and national government positions.

The road to freedom has not proved an easy one for minorities who still struggle for equality today, but the Emancipation Proclamation must be credited for the turning of the tide. Whether a political or a moral move, the decision to issue the Emancipation Proclamation was made by a man who, according to the document, "sincerely believed ['it'] to be an act of justice."

Perspectives on the Proclamation

Within a group of four or five students, discuss the following questions based on the student reading. Elect a secretary to record your group's responses on a separate sheet of paper.

1. How does the student reading argue that the Emancipation Proclamation was at least in part a military move?

2. Does the Constitution outlaw secession from the Union?

3. Which slaves were freed by the Emancipation Proclamation? What legal act or document freed all other slaves in the United States in 1865?

4. Lincoln was easily elected to the presidency on the anti-slavery stand he took in the Lincoln-Douglas debates. Why did he wait until 1863 to confront the slavery issue—and even then only to free slaves in the rebellious states?

5. Even though it did not free all slaves in the United States, the Emancipation Proclamation is a significant historical document. Why?

6. Within the text of the Emancipation Proclamation, President Lincoln said:

   > And I hereby enjoin upon the people so declared to
   > be free to abstain from all violence, unless in
   > necessary self-defense; and I recommend to them
   > that, in all cases where allowed, they labor
   > faithfully for reasonable wages.

   Are sufficient jobs available today to minorities in our country that offer "reasonable wages"? Do migrant workers and unskilled laborers obtain "reasonable wages"? Does today's minimum wage support a family?

Slavery to the Tenth Degree

The Emancipation Proclamation is one of several documents and decisions from around the world of the nineteenth and twentieth centuries that marked a change in attitudes toward enslavement, personal freedom, and human equality. Today's political leaders and common people are in accord with the United Nation's 1948 Universal Declaration of Human Rights, which condemns slavery. Still economic, political, and social enslavement is a reality around the globe.

Listed below are enslaving situations from the past and present. Rank them from least to most restrictive with absolute slavery being most restrictive (as indicated with the number 10), and political, social, and economic inequities characterizing the less restrictive. Be prepared to justify your rankings to the rest of the class.

_____ Rank

An African citizen is captured by another African citizen in 1650 and sold to a transporter who loads the prisoner on a ship with hundreds of others who are taken to the colony of Virginia and sold as property to a plantation owner who, although somewhat "regulated" by law, can brand, chain, or even mutilate him if he does not perform the physical labor demanded of him by his master.

_____ Rank

Blacks in South Africa lived under Apartheid from 1948 through 1991. Laws prohibited them from holding public office, residing in white neighborhoods, or marrying outside of their race. In addition, blacks were required to carry identification cards at all times and to seek permission before leaving the townships in which they had been forced to settle.

_____ Rank

Migrant workers pick crops in the United States in return for sometimes inadequate room and board and minimum or less than minimum wage. Impoverished and poorly educated, unable to find year-round work in one location, these laborers ride buses or vans from one region of the country to another as crops mature and workers are needed for harvest.

_____ Rank

Under the system of Peonage, seventeenth-century Native Americans in Spanish colonies including Mexico, were virtually enslaved in mines and on plantations. Unable to leave a job until debts were paid, required to buy staples in company stores at inflated prices, and saddled with all the accumulated debts of parents and grandparents, the peons were trapped in an inescapable misery almost until the twentieth century.

_____ Rank

Workers in a clothing factory in modern-day Saipan in the western Pacific cut textiles for 18 hours a day before being locked in company barracks for the night. As in much of the "sweatshop" garment industry in the United States, wages are extremely low.

_____ Rank

Serfs of the Middle Ages were required by law to work the land owned by their lord or nobleman. Although allowed to own a bit of their own land and permitted to buy their freedom, few serfs could afford to even support their families due to the heavy, arbitrary taxes they were required to pay their lords. From peasantry and serfdom there was no escape but death which came early under such harsh conditions.

_____ Rank

The craft guilds that were the economic basis of cities in the Middle Ages divided skilled workers into three classes: masters, journeymen, and apprentices. While a master owned his business, journeymen worked for very low wages and under severe conditions, and apprentices received nothing more than a bed in the master's house for their services. Tight restrictions made it virtually impossible for journeymen to become masters, and both they and apprentices were subjected to whatever treatment their masters saw fit for keeping them in line and controlling profits in the business.

_____ Rank

More than two million American children under the age of 16—some as young as three years—worked in factories, farms, mines, and mills at the turn of the century as the Industrial Revolution demanded lots of cheap labor. Conditions were crowded, dirty, and hazardous. Children worked as many as 15 hours a day running mechanical looms, sewing coats, canning fruit, picking vegetables, and mining coal.

_____ Rank

Prisoners in Nazi Germany's concentration camps were literally worked to death in chemical and industrial factories. Camp conditions were atrocious. Prisoners were deprived of adequate food, water, clothing, and housing. Camp authorities abused inmates, and more than six million prisoners no longer healthy or young enough to work the endless hours that were required of them were put to death.

_____ Rank

To pay for their months' long passage to America, millions of early immigrants became indentured servants. Owners of the contracts often treated the indentured servants harshly, making the four- to seven-year terms of service a virtual slavery, but at the end they received new clothes, a gun, a plot of land, and citizenship. In this servitude were both "free-willers" and involuntary immigrants—convicts or kidnap victims or exiles from their home countries. This practice has reemerged recently with modern human smuggling, especially of Asians desperate to enter America.

I Didn't Know That!

Test your American Civil War I.Q. by determining which of the following statements about the war and the time period are true and which are false. An answer key provides explanations for the correct answers.

_____ 1. Because the United States Constitution stipulates that Congress alone can adopt amendments, President Lincoln did not officially approve the Thirteenth Amendment.

_____ 2. President Lincoln once considered slaves property.

_____ 3. Northern states supported the federal government more loyally than Southern states even before the Civil War began.

_____ 4. On October 16, 1859, John Brown and his followers raided a federal armory because they opposed the strong federal government.

_____ 5. In 1860 the president of the United States stated that he would not forcibly prevent any state from seceding from the Union.

_____ 6. At the end of the Civil War, plantation owners were stripped of their property which was given to the slaves that farmed the land.

_____ 7. Vice President Andrew Johnson, who was launched into the presidency following Abraham Lincoln's assassination, was impeached and removed from office in 1868.

_____ 8. The 1964 Civil Rights Act was preceded by a Civil Rights Act passed by Congress 100 years earlier.

_____ 9. African Americans were not permitted to run for public office immediately following the Civil War.

_____ 10. Freed persons in the South were able to make a new life only after the republicans who first took charge after the Civil War were voted out of office by the democrats who created the Freedmen's Bureau to help establish schools, create employment, and protect blacks from violence and fraud.

_____ 11. Twenty-three African-American soldiers were awarded the Medal of Honor for bravery following the Civil War.

_____ 12. The centennial of the signing of the Emancipation Proclamation was celebrated by the NAACP with the passage of the Civil Rights Act.

And the March Goes On

Although the Emancipation Proclamation was signed in 1863 and the Fourteenth Amendment ratified in 1865, minorities continue to struggle for equality in the United States today. Consider the following hurdles to justice described below and identify the act or situation that got us over the hurdle. Place the letter of the solution on the blank beside the number of the hurdle it solved.

HURDLE

_____ 1. African citizens are captured to be sold as slaves in the colonies.

_____ 2. Slaves are forced to toil the land, provide domestic services, and work in the trade industry.

_____ 3. Former slaves need jobs and schools to be assimilated into the free society.

_____ 4. Southern democrats pass "black codes" limiting black occupations and property rights and justifying forced labor for "unemployable" adults and "unsupervised" youths.

_____ 5. Black citizens cannot legally vote.

_____ 6. Black citizens attend inferior schools.

_____ 7. Segregation ordinances direct blacks to the backs of theaters and buses and to separate drinking fountains, public restrooms, and restaurant tables.

_____ 8. Minority men and women are passed over for new jobs, job promotions, and raises. They are paid less than their white, male counterparts in the work world.

_____ 9. Nearly 50% of the U.S. prison population is black.

SOLUTION

A. The Freedmen's Bureau establishes schools and provides other services to former slaves.

B. The Fifteenth Amendment is ratified.

C. Affirmative Action laws attempt to compensate for past discrimination, especially in the workplace.

D. Rosa Parks refuses to give up her seat, a wave of sit-ins begin, Martin Luther King, Jr., speaks eloquently, and the Civil Rights Act of 1964 responds to the public outcry for justice.

E. The Thirteenth Amendment is ratified.

F. A U.S. law bans the importation of slaves.

G. The Fourteenth Amendment guarantees that U.S. citizenship rights apply to all citizens.

H. Chief Justice Earl Warren decides in the *Brown* v. *Board of Education* case that separate schools are not equal schools.

I. Justice system reform and attention to social issues including deteriorating urban conditions must address this modern hurdle.

The Communist Manifesto

Background

Background

In the mid-1880s, Karl Marx and Fredrich Engels were commissioned by the Communist League—a secret organization of German intellectuals—to write a platform statement for their political group. The resulting *Communist Manifesto* outlines Marx's theory of history, criticizes capitalists and previous socialist models of reform, and predicts an eventual end to the class structure of societies.

Decidedly the most influential document in movements opposing capitalism, the *Communist Manifesto* has served as the driving force behind the development of socialist and communist governments worldwide. Yet traditional Marxists contend that the repressive communist societies of China and Cuba are anything but Marxist, and that the modern-day socialist nations with existing bourgeois structures oppose the spirit and principles of the *Manifesto*.

The *Communist Manifesto* advocates a single, universal society of democracy based on a classless equality. Marx believed democracy not to be possible in societies governed by dictators who force communist principles upon the masses. He believed democracy not to be possible in socialist societies that offer welfare assistance and improved working conditions to employees in lieu of real power. He believed democracy not to be possible in capitalistic societies where rich owners of the means of production retain the economic and political clout. Marx predicted that true democracy would one day be accomplished only when the working class rose against the property and means-of-production owners and overthrew the entire system worldwide in favor of a classless society of individuals working—not for personal profit but for the good of the universal society.

In this lesson students learn about the historical significance of the *Communist Manifesto* as they discover how its message has been adulterated and misinterpreted by capitalists and communists alike in attempts by world leaders and political parties to navigate the course of history. The student reading is a fictitious preface to a one hundred and fiftieth anniversary edition of the *Manifesto*—a document that has been translated and reprinted countless times since its penning in 1848. The student activity that follows the *Manifesto* preface encourages reflections on the reading, while other activities and extensions focus on the history of capitalism, the successes and failures of communal societies, socialist thinkers other than Marx, and the similarities and differences between communism, socialism, capitalism, and other socio-economic structures.

Teaching Activities

Marxism for Democrats

Students reflect on the viewpoints stated in the student reading in answering the thought-provoking questions in this activity.

Will Work for Profit

In this activity, students gain an understanding of capitalism as they study its history and principles.

Communal Living

Students discover Marxism in practice as they explore historical communes.

Socialist Thinkers' Thoughts

Students study the views of socialist philosophers other than Marx in this activity.

Socio-Economic Alternatives

Students compare and contrast various modern-day and historical socio-economic systems from around the world.

Extensions

1. The 23-page German pamphlet of 1848, the *Communist Manifesto*, has been translated into English, Polish, French, Italian, Spanish, Russian, Danish, and Swedish, with new editions in several languages being published periodically to meet the demands of its market. Marx and Engels wrote interesting prefaces and additional notes for editions that came out later, acknowledging changes in history but standing by the document's principles, predictions, and significance. With your class, read the document in its entirety. Discuss individual student interpretations of the four sections of the *Manifesto* and then assign each of four groups of students to rewrite one of the sections of the document in modern-day language.

2. Read fictional accounts of what it might be like to live in a utopian community in one of these classic accounts: *Utopia* by Sir Thomas More, *New Atlantis* by Francis Bacon, *Oceana* by James Harrington, *Erchwon* by Samuel Butler, *Modern Utopia* by H.G. Wells, *Walden Two* by B.F. Skinner.

3. Continue your study of Marx, the man, and the Marxist theories by researching Karl Marx in the library or on the Internet. Works written by Marx include *Critique of Political Economy* (1859), *Das Kapital: Volume One* (1867), *The Civil War in France* (1871), *The Gotha Program* (1875), and *Das Kapital: Volumes Two and Three* (1885 and 1894—posthumous, edited by Engels).

4. Study the life and works of Fredrich Engels, the coauthor of the *Communist Manifesto*, the editor of the second and third volumes of Karl Marx' *Das Kapital*, and an interesting and influential revolutionary in his own right. In addition to the writings he collaborated on with Marx, Engels wrote newspaper articles and books independently on topics ranging from politics and economics to physical science and anthropology. He even financially supported Marx with monies he earned working at a textile mill.

COMMUNIST MANIFESTO

A One Hundred Fiftieth Anniversary English Edition

Preface

Countless editions of Karl Marx and Fredrich Engels' 1848 *Communist Manifesto* have been issued over the past 150 years. Originally written as a platform statement of the secret German Communist League, it has become the impetus for socialist and communist movements the world over. Lenin came to power in the name of the *Manifesto*. Stalin killed his enemies in the name of the *Manifesto*. Castro dictates the social conditions of his entire citizenry in the name of the *Manifesto*. Yet Lenin, Stalin, and Castro-style communism have little in common with the communism of Marx.

What Marx Did Not Say

The conventional definition of communism evokes images of Stalin's Great Purge and Deng's massacre of student protesters at Tiananmen Square. Modern communist governments create repressive conditions in which the state controls both properties and lives. Communist leaders like to cite the *Communist Manifesto* as their source of authority, suggesting that they are leading movements that will free workers and common people from the evils of capitalism as Marx predicted would one day happen. Yet Marx did not condone any form of authoritarian rule and believed that "the emancipation of workers must be the act of the working class itself."

According to a footnote at the end of Section One of the *Communist Manifesto*, Marx's communism referred to "village communities" like those "found to have been the primitive form of society everywhere from India to Ireland," the dissolution of which produced societies "differentiated into separate and finally antagonistic classes." Communism, to Marx, signified the end of all class struggles and the "raising of the proletariat to the position of ruling class to win the battle of democracy."

What Marx Did Say

The *Communist Manifesto* serves as the most precise source of Marx's theories and predictions about history, politics, economics, and society. Divided into four sections, the first outlines Marx's theory of the evolution of societies, suggesting that the "history of all hitherto society is the history of class struggles." The section reviews past struggles—from those of the slaves and freemen in ancient Rome to those of the serfs and lords of the Middle Ages—and suggests that the emergence of the current class struggle between the bourgeoisie (capitalists) and the proletariat (workers) grew out of the expansion of trade and industrial production that doomed the feudal system and ushered in the age of capitalism. Marx suggests that the capitalists' "need of a constantly expanding market for its products chases the bourgeoisie over the entire surface of the globe," as an ever-increasing number of workers are paid less and less to produce more and more until the laborer can no longer afford the products he makes and "what the bourgeoisie (eventually) produce, above all, are its own gravediggers."

Believing that the bourgeoisie of his day "had stripped of its halo every occupation hitherto honored and looked up to with reverent awe" and left the proletariat in a condition of being no more than "a commodity, like every other article of commerce . . . an appendage of the machine," Marx predicted in Section Two that laborers would rise against the land and means-of-production owners worldwide to abolish private property and to create a classless society of direct, democratic rule.

In the third section, Marx criticizes other socialist movements and theories, and in the fourth he defines communist tactics and calls for the unity of workers everywhere.

The Significance of Marx's Philosophy

Marx and Engels predicted the *Communist Manifesto* would "do for history what Darwin's theory has done for biology" and so were loath to modify the later editions of the document even when significant historical changes prompted Engels to write in the preface of the 1872 German version that "this programme has in some details been antiquated." Instead of changing the document itself, Engels prefaced later editions with the notice that "the practical application of the principles will depend . . . on the historical conditions for the time being existing" and even suggested "that the revolutionary measures proposed at the end of Section Two . . . would, in many respects, be very differently worded today."

So where does Marxian philosophy stand as we approach the year 2000? Does his class struggle theory of history still ring true? Is his prediction of an end to the class structure of societies any closer to coming true than it was at the height of the Industrial Revolution?

One hundred fifty years later, the *Communist Manifesto* warrants another look. It is significant in its theories and its predictions, as well as in its historical corruptions that contributed to the rise and fall of Communist Russia and continue to claim power in China. The publishers of this one hundred fiftieth anniversary edition of the *Communist Manifesto* suggest capitalists, socialists, and communists alike revisit the immortal words and ideas of Karl Marx.

Marxism for Democrats

On a separate sheet of paper, answer in complete sentences the following questions based on the student reading.

1. According to the student reading, how did capitalism come to exist? Do you agree with Marx that all history is the history of class struggles? Do you believe a classless society will ever cover the entire planet? Dominate a single nation?

2. Karl Marx believed that a direct democracy wherein all members of society enjoy equal rights and powers was not possible in the presence of capitalism. Why did he believe capitalism stood in the way of true democracy? Do you believe democracy and capitalism can coexist?

3. According to the student reading, how does Marx's definition of *communism* differ from the conventional definition of the word? Why would Marx not consider Cuba, China, or the former USSR and Eastern bloc countries communist?

4. According to the student reading, Marx did not advocate a working class revolution, but rather predicted one. In Section Two of the *Manifesto*, he outlined in ten broad steps the general process that the move from capitalism to Marxist communism might take. Can you cite examples of any of these (paraphrased) planks happening to any degree in America today?

   Plank One: Abolition of private property
   Plank Two: Heavy income tax
   Plank Three: Abolition of rights of inheritance
   Plank Four: Confiscation of bourgeois property
   Plank Five: Establishment of a national bank
   Plank Six: Centralized communication and transportation
   Plank Seven: Increase in state-owned factories
   Plank Eight: Requirement that all citizens be workers
   Plank Nine: Population becomes equally distributed
   Plank Ten: Education is provided free by state

5. Marx suggested that one of the reasons that a workers' revolution was slow in developing was that workers could not unite because they were pitted against one another due to nationalism and capitalism. How might the existence of separate countries throughout the world be seen as separating workers? How does capitalism pit worker against worker?

6. Although Marx promoted the abolition of private property, he was not referring to the "hard-won, self-acquired self-earned property" of the "petty artisan and the small peasant" but to the property of the bourgeois class. How do the tools of a carpenter and the land of a small-scale farmer differ from the corporations, industrial complexes, and extensive real estate owned by wealthy capitalists?

Will Work for Profit

How much do you know about the socio-economic system in place in your own nation? Test your capitalism I.Q. with the true/false quiz.

T   F   1. *Capitalism* refers to an economic system in which businesses are owned privately and products are sold on the open market for profit.

T   F   2. Capitalism reached its zenith in the 1960s.

T   F   3. The Father of Capitalism title belongs to John Adams.

T   F   4. *Capital* generally refers to the buildings, equipment, land, etc., needed to produce goods.

T   F   5. Supply and demand as well as competition with other producers of the same goods dictate prices in a capitalist society.

T   F   6. Proponents of capitalism believe competitive markets and the self-interest of entrepreneurs will benefit society as a whole.

T   F   7. *Capital* can be defined as goods and monies that can produce future income.

T   F   8. Capitalists get rich because they never have to put profits back into the system.

T   F   9. Traditional capitalists, such as Adam Smith, demanded strong government regulations to protect the interests of their industries.

T   F   10. The original intent of capitalism was to allow small businesses to blossom into large corporations that could monopolize an entire industry.

T   F   11. The Great Depression exemplifies the largest flaw in capitalistic societies—their tendency to create periods of "boom and bust."

T   F   12. All modern-day democracies operate within a capitalist socio-economic system.

Communal Living

At the time of Marx, the terms *socialism* and *communism* were expressions of hope and idealism, born in the belief that in the right circumstances people could live and work and prosper together happily without exploitation, brutality, or want. Experiments in utopian communities throughout history have ranged from the religious to the authoritarian to the anarchistic. In fiction a utopia lasts forever, but in reality, communes are imperfect. Read the capsule descriptions of real "utopias" given here; then guess which communities continue to exist today and determine what factors lasting communities share.

Hutterian Brethren: This religious sect of pacifists, whose belief in the common ownership of property and opposition to politics made them outsiders, began in what is today the Czech Republic in the early 1500s. Their leader was burned at the stake as a heretic, and they migrated eventually to America, where they settled in Montana and the Dakotas and insisted on speaking only German.

Shakers: Originally known as the Shaking Quakers, these spiritualists gave up private interests and property to "the service of God," practiced strict celibacy, believed they had power over disease, and trusted that their leaders were preparing a kingdom on earth for the Second Coming. They had as many as 20 farming villages in the Northeast United States by 1826, but they never bore children to replenish their numbers. Their crafts and architecture stressed simple functionalism over beauty and adornment.

Amish: In the latter part of the seventeenth century, these devoutly religious people who practiced excommunication as a means of church discipline settled in Pennsylvania. They shunned modern technology from buttons to electricity, preferring simple farming lives. Refusing to vote, to serve in the military, or to let their children be educated beyond the eighth grade, they forbade marriage to outsiders. Although nonviolent themselves, the Amish were thought subversive and widely persecuted.

Oneida Community: Founded in 1848 in upstate New York, this experiment in utopian society made a practice of "multiple marriage" and "selfish love," strongly discouraging monogamous romantic attachments. Conception of children was scientifically planned, and their rearing was accomplished by the entire community. Manufacturing, science, and engineering were priorities, and members changed occupations frequently so as to master many trades. They advocated perfectionism and Bible "communism." According to their founder, "the sin-system, the marriage-system, the work-system, and the death-system were all one, and must be abolished together."

Morning Star Ranch: In 1966 Lou Gottlieb, a Bay Area musician, caught up in the hippie spirit of the time, turned his property north of San Francisco into an open commune. Primitive of religion, characterized by free love, nudism, and hallucinogenic drugs, modest farming was accomplished, but little else. Runaways, winos, tourists, bikers, and hippies lived in tents, huts, tepees, and even a hollowed-out redwood stump equipped with a flat roof. Tribal in nature and devoid of rules, Morning Star may have established a historic zenith of utter anarchy. When charged by the health department with running an organized camp without sufficient sanitary facilities, Gottlieb commented, "If they find any evidence of organization here, I wish they would show it to me."

Fruitlands: In Harvard, Massachusetts, in 1841, a small farm community was begun by two American intellectuals. Striving for kindliness, purity, and simplicity, this commune rejected the ideas of trading, of using animals for work, of eating animal products or drinking anything but water, or of belonging to any religion. All emphasis was on *being* rather than on *doing*. One of the members was a transcendentalist who survived an entire year on crackers and a second year entirely on apples. Another resident advocated nudism, even in harsh winter.

New Harmony: The world-famous industrialist Robert Owen, in 1825, bought an entire town in Indiana and bankrolled his new commune with the fortune he brought with him from England. Launched with great fanfare, New Harmony promised to be a "halfway house," a socialist 30,000-acre farming community readying its 900 residents for true and ideal communism. There was no religious worship, but Owen's financial support paid for free education, free prescription drugs, free band concerts and dances, plus five military companies. After announcing the first constitution in New Harmony, Owen departed to Europe for a year. When he returned, he decided a different constitution was in order. Before the second year was over, Owen found need to completely rewrite the document another five times.

Monastic Living: Religious individuals who vow to abandon the world and devote themselves to God exist in the Christian, Hindu, Buddhist, and Islam religions. Individual monastic communities hold differing rules pertaining to dress, poverty, charity work, prayer, worship, religious studies, and solitude, but each insists on their members' commitment to God and disregard for worldly concerns.

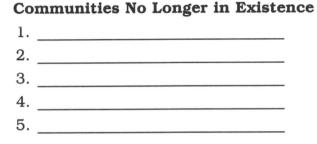

Communities That Continue to Exist

1. _____
2. _____
3. _____

Communities No Longer in Existence

1. _____
2. _____
3. _____
4. _____
5. _____

Things to Consider . . .

1. What do the communities that continue to exist today have in common?
2. What do the communities that no longer exist have in common?

Things to Research . . .

1. Locate books on communes in your school library and read more about a commune of your choice.
2. Read about the history of communes in general including information on primitive societies.

Things to Write About . . .

On your own sheet of paper, write an essay using one of the following titles:

Primal Living: Primitive Communities from the Past and Present

Can't We All Just Get Along? Why Communes Fail

Communes Spanning History: What Makes Lasting Communes Last?

A Day in the Life of (Founder's Name): An In-depth Look at (Name of Commune)

Socialist Thinkers' Thoughts

Below are brief summaries of the views of several socialist thinkers, parties, or societies who were either influenced by or influenced the writings and philosophies of Marx. Choose one thinker or group to research and write about. At one point in your report, compare and contrast the socialist view you researched with the socialist view of Karl Marx.

1. **Eduard Bernstein (1850-1932):** This friend of Fredrich Engels agreed that a communal system of ownership and democratic rule constituted an ideal society but suggested that a revolution was not necessary to realize this goal. His book, *Evolutionary Socialism*, predicted that socialism would evolve naturally over time.

2. **Robert Owen (1771-1858):** This utopian socialist believed that humankind as a whole would profit from improved working and living conditions for individuals and improved working conditions for factory employees. He established a trade union in Britain and conducted an experiment in communal living in the United States.

3. **The Fabian Society:** This group of British middle class intellectuals did not agree with Marx's class struggle theory of history; members believed peaceful changes could bring about the collective ownership and control of a country's resources.

4. **Eugene Victor Debs (1855-1926):** Mr. Debs organized the Social Democratic Party of America after reading Marx's *Das Kapital* while imprisoned for leading a strike of the American Railroad Union. He ran for United States president four times. His 1920 election campaign was run from a jail cell where he found himself imprisoned for criticizing American involvement in World War I. A reputed man of principle and integrity, even those opposed to his views respected Mr. Debs.

5. **Comte de Claude Henri de Rouvroy Saint-Simon:** One of the founders of modern socialism, Saint-Simon fought in the American and French Revolutions. He believed that industry and science guided by Christian principles could eliminate poverty and promote improved social conditions for all classes of people.

6. **Salvador Allende Gossens (1908-1973):** Chilean president from 1970 to 1973, Gossens attempted to nationalize industries and improve working conditions in his country. When a United States-supported rebellion threatened his position, he committed suicide.

7. **Labour Party:** This political party supports candidates for Great Britain Parliament who represent the concerns of the working class and trade unions.

8. **Norman Mattoon Thomas (1884-1968):** This United States Socialist Party six-time candidate for president spoke out against totalitarianism. He believed industry should create products as needed in society rather than for profit. He worked to create a minimum wage, unemployment insurance, and child labor laws.

9. **Vladimir Ilyich Lenin (1870-1924):** After studying *Das Kapital*, Lenin recruited professional revolutionaries with Leon Trotsky and overthrew Russia's czar and established the USSR. Not certain how to create a workers' state, Lenin resorted to a New Economic Policy in 1921 that created a mixed economy of government and privately owned and operated businesses. In an attempt to maintain his power, Lenin eventually insisted on a one-party political system.

Socio-Economic Alternatives

Human beings have lived under myriad socio-economic systems throughout history. Write the letter of the definition on the right beside the correct system listed on the left. Hint: Root words in the system's terms may provide a clue to their definitions.

_____ 1. Mercantilism

_____ 2. Capitalism

_____ 3. Communism

_____ 4. Socialism

_____ 5. Totalitarianism

_____ 6. Nationalism

_____ 7. Marxism

_____ 8. Imperialism

A. Total control of the social, economic, political, cultural, and educational conditions of the state are entrusted to the state's rulers.

B. Sixteenth- to eighteenth-century European economic philosophy that suggested national strength was based on exports outnumbering imports

C. Although never fully realized, this socio-economic theory of communal living has found limited success with the Hutterian Brethren among others.

D. This economic system assumes that private ownership and the open market will encourage growth and production that will benefit the entire state.

E. The nation began to define the social and cultural identities of its citizens with the spread of the Industrial Revolution and the development of separate national identities.

F. A social system of state-operated production and state-distributed wealth arrived at through legislative decisions within a previously capitalistic system

G. A situation in which capitalist nations exercise economic and/or political influence over weaker countries

H. A communal society of joint ownership of resources and means of production arrived at through revolution

The New Deal Legislation

On March 4, 1933, Franklin D. Roosevelt took over the helm of a country in which factories were closing, banks were going under, commodity prices were plummeting, and 16 million people were unemployed. President Roosevelt responded to the economic crisis immediately, initiating the "first hundred days," the period from March 9 through June 16 when he encouraged through strong leadership the passage of legislation to relieve victims of the Great Depression. The programs, agencies, services, regulations, and subsidies he implemented during those first months in office and on through the year 1939 are called Roosevelt's New Deal.

Although the "Brain Trust," a group of lawyers, professors, and professionals who advised the president, had no central economic philosophy, and many hastily written acts they suggested were subsequently struck down as unconstitutional, the New Deal did change the course of American social and economic history. It established centralized control of the economy and created a "welfare state" in which social security, unemployment, federally funded housing, (Aid to Families with Dependent Children), and numerous other programs and agencies provided a safety net that insured social economic security for all United States residents.

The philosophy that the federal government is responsible for providing its citizens with an economic safety net is well-founded in history. England instituted Poor Laws in the 1500s authorizing districts to collect taxes for the relief of the poor, to provide unemployment payments to those unable to work, and to create workhouses for the able-bodied. Nearly all modern democratic societies accept the responsibility for the social and economic well-being of their residents. Yet the approach to solving the problems of poverty, homelessness, and unemployment in the United States has recently come into question in light of the rising cost of social security and a number of exposed cases of welfare fraud and abuse.

In this lesson students read a review of a book that asks the question, "Who is responsible for the care of this nation's elderly, disabled, unemployed, homeless, and poor?" Through activities and extension projects, students clarify their own ideas regarding the welfare debate, take a closer look at FDR's New Deal legislation and its modern-day counterparts, research the life and times of both Franklin and Eleanor Roosevelt, and create a time line of Franklin D. Roosevelt's remarkable presidency.

Teaching Activities

Reviewing the Review

Students make their own judgments about how best the country can "promote the general welfare" as they answer these questions based on the student reading.

What's Left of the New Deal?

Students acknowledge the number of current programs and policies that owe their existence to New Deal legislation with this activity.

Rules and Regulations

Students examine the role of various government commissions and agencies.

Putting It in Perspective

President Roosevelt was in office during two of the most challenging periods in United States history: the Great Depression years and World War II. With this activity, students put it all in perspective as they place significant events of the era on a time line.

Extensions

1. Eleanor Roosevelt earned two unofficial titles during her 12 years in the White House: "First Lady of the World" and "Eleanor Everywhere." The first title reflected her hard-working determination to improve conditions for people of every land, and the second reflected her willingness to jump into a plane and travel anywhere to do so. As Franklin was confined to a wheelchair, Eleanor served as his legs, greeting military personnel abroad, inspecting state hospitals and prisons, and inviting surprise guests to dinner—poor farmers and factory workers whom she seated beside her husband at the White House dinner table where they discussed their plight in the midst of the Great Depression. The stories of Eleanor Roosevelt are extraordinary and numerous. She worked for justice and social reform well into her senior years when President Truman—who succeeded her husband following his death— appointed her as the first United States delegate to the United Nations.

Compose a biography of Eleanor Roosevelt by assigning groups of students to research her childhood, her personal life, and her commitment to the American people and the people of all nations in her role as "First Lady of the World."

2. Franklin D. Roosevelt spent 12 years as president of the United States. However, his road to the presidency was filled with fascinating bumps and curves. Study and report on FDR's pre-president years.

3. Franklin D. Roosevelt assisted the downtrodden during the years of the Great Depression by pushing his New Deal legislation through Congress. Assign research and reports on other humanitarians who have worked on behalf of the elderly, poor, sick, or hungry. Students may wish to report on Mother Teresa and her work in Calcutta, Albert Schweitzer and his African hospital, or Father Flanagan's establishment of Boys Town.

4. The 1929 crash of the stock market led to the Great Depression of the early 1930s. Research and report on the causes of the 1929 stock market crash.

5. Social workers fill positions in many of the agencies created under New Deal policies. Research the jobs available to social workers, the amount of training required for the various positions, and the amount of money a social worker can expect to earn. Are social worker positions dwindling or increasing with modern reforms in the welfare system?

6. Research the country's social security system. What types of income are taxed to support the system? Who receives benefits and at what levels? Who administers the system? How much money is in the system? Can future generations depend on the funds to support them in their old age?

WELFARE STATE

by James Dees
Reader's Press $21.99

In his latest book, James Dees, renowned social commentator, poses the question, "Who is responsible for the care of this nation's elderly, disabled, unemployed, homeless, and poor?" According to Dees, although nearly all modern democratic nations accept responsibility for the social and economic well-being of their residents, a universal questioning of the philosophy behind the welfare state is currently emerging not only here in the United States, but also in France, Canada, Germany, and England as budgetary crises erode social safety nets once assumed to be permanent.

In the first section of his book, Dees outlines the history of the welfare state. He highlights the traumatic shift in European economies from agriculturally-based feudal systems to modern industrial states. He also cites the wrenching experiences of the peasants who were displaced from their farms; divorced from their feudal lords who once provided support in times of famine, sickness, and disability; and thrust into an urban existence working for pitiful wages in sweltering and dangerous mines, mills, and factories. Grim early photographs, political cartoons, and journal entries of the eighteenth and nineteenth centuries attest to the sufferings of beggars and vagabonds who were flogged, branded, condemned to slavery, and even executed and to women and children (as young as five years of age) chained to machines they tended from before dawn until midnight.

Slowly European states responded to the atrocities. Reformers in the nineteenth century managed to get laws passed that limited the work day of women and children to ten hours. Germany provided social insurance to the sick in 1883 and to the elderly in 1889. Great Britain followed suit in 1911, New Zealand in 1938, and Australia in the 1930s and 1940s.

The birth of the United States' welfare system is explored in this section of Dees' book as well. A thorough history of the Great Depression provides the background for Franklin D. Roosevelt's New Deal legislation. Workers' marches, union strikes, farmers' refusals to transport foods into cities until paid a livable wage, soup lines, grocery store break-ins, and Herbert Hoover's orders to burn down a camp of World War I veterans set up on Capital Hill demonstrate the panicky mood of a nation on the verge of a worker rebellion in 1933 when President Roosevelt took over the helm.

The 1935 Social Security Act and the numerous pieces of legislation to follow are seen as bold and necessary programs for the restoration of order in the nation. According to Dees, the government's willingness to protect its citizens from unbridled capitalism with its ruthless business practices, devastating cycles of bust and boom, and wild financial speculations reestablished faith in the banking and exchange systems, provided relief and jobs to the nation's millions of unemployed and bankrupt citizens, and saved the country. Although many New Deal acts were eventually struck down as unconstitutional, Roosevelt engraved on America the philosophy that the federal government is responsible for what happens in the workplace, the family, and the economy as a whole.

The prohibitive cost of maintaining the benefits of unemployment checks, medical coverage, AFDC, food stamps, and other government "entitlements" that can be traced to New Deal legislation is cited in the final section of Dees' book as the cause of the questioning of the welfare state philosophy today. The payroll tax that supports Social Security has jumped from 2% at the time of its inception to 13% today. Widespread welfare fraud has been documented in the media. And critics contend that entitlement programs undermine the work ethic and the family structure itself.

Various political parties, civil rights organizations, and advocates for the poor answer Dees' original question about who is responsible for the poor in different ways. State- and city-managed welfare-to-work programs that provide welfare recipients with everything from subsidized child care to career counseling and scheduled job interviews are said to pit low-income workers against those just entering the work world from the welfare rolls. Government-funded social service networks operated by area churches may provide spiritual hope as well as material necessities, but adversaries contend that the "charitable choice" clause that makes such cooperation between church and state possible is unconstitutional. Welfare reform acts of the 1980s and 1990s that force welfare recipients to enroll in job training programs and threaten to severely limit the amount of time one can collect food stamps and other federal financial assistance address the budget problem but ignore the underlying economic structure that creates the need for General and Emergency Assistance in the first place.

James Dees does not profess to have the solution to the welfare question today, but he pulls no punches as he demonstrates that capitalistic, industrialized systems operating on competition and trade in more and more merchandise somehow need to bridle greed and take the responsibility for the care of their own elderly, disabled, unemployed, homeless, and poor. Our nation's very Constitution, Dees reminds us, promises that the government will "insure domestic tranquility" and "promote the general welfare."

Reviewing the Review

How would you answer James Dees' question of "Who is responsible for the care of this nation's elderly, disabled, unemployed, homeless, and poor?" On your own paper answer in complete sentences the following questions based on the student reading.

1. While some political scientists, economists, and sociologists suggest that a government-supported safety net needs to be built into the American system to handle the "excesses of capitalism," others contend that welfare for anyone except the severely disabled or aged encourages laziness and is anti-capitalistic in nature. With which view do you more closely align?

2. To what degree is poverty a result of social and economic problems in a society?

3. New Deal legislation was aimed at employing the unemployed, relieving the bankrupt, restoring confidence in the banking system and the stock market, and otherwise rebuilding America following the greatest economic depression this nation has yet known. Do you think Roosevelt meant for the programs and policies he established to continue indefinitely? Has the fact that many of his programs have continued so long been good or bad for America?

4. Some welfare reform critics contend that offering subsidized child care, free bus passes, and reading and math tutoring to welfare recipients (and a $2,100 tax break to employers who hire them) creates an unfair playing field for low-income earners who compete for unskilled labor jobs. How could welfare reform be handled in such a way that does not pit poor workers against poor welfare recipients?

5. What might the Constitution's preamble have meant by declaring that the establishment of the document was in part "in order to insure domestic tranquility" and "promote the general welfare"?

6. Would it be possible to set up a country in such a way that it would never see poverty and hunger? If so, what political, social, and economic systems would ensure that a class of needy citizens would never arise? Even if a country claimed 0% unemployment, 0% homelessness, and 0% hunger with its general population, it would still possess sick, injured, and elderly citizens, in addition to young children who could not support themselves through gainful employment. Is a society as a whole responsible for supporting its members who cannot support themselves? If so, how best might this be achieved?

7. Do you believe church-administered, federally funded welfare-to-work systems to be unconstitutional? What are the pros and cons of this arrangement?

What's Left of the New Deal?

New Deal legislation set a precedent in America for centralized control of the economy and federal funding to promote the general welfare. Although many of the acts FDR pushed through Congress were later struck down as unconstitutional, several programs, subsidies, and policies that were enacted from 1933 to 1939 continue to exist today in modified form either under their original name or under a new one. Research which of the following New Deal programs, agencies, acts, and regulations continue to be operable today. Mark operable programs with an "O" and nonoperable programs with an "N.O."

_____ 1. Fair Labor Standards Act

This act originally set a minimum wage of $.25 per hour and an overtime pay scale at time and a half for time worked beyond 44 hours per week. It also prohibited oppressive child labor. The act has been amended many times to increase the minimum wage and prohibit different pay for men and women.

_____ 2. National Labor Relations Act

This act gave legal protection to workers joining labor unions and engaging in collective bargaining for improved wages or working conditions.

_____ 3. Social Security Act

This act designates funding and programs that provide unemployed, sick, disabled, and elderly citizens with medical subsidies and needed income. Social Security programs are funded through a tax on income.

_____ 4. Agricultural Adjustment Act of 1933

Under this act farmers were paid by the federal government to limit their production of certain crops and livestock.

_____ 5. Public Works Administration

This agency was set up to provide funds for the construction of roads and buildings.

_____ 6. Securities and Exchange Commission

Created by the Security and Exchange Act of 1934 to restore public faith in the stock market, this commission regulates trade in securities.

_____ 7. Rural Electrification Administration

This agency was established to help provide electricity and phone service to rural areas by providing low-interest loans to individuals and organizations.

_____ 8. National Recovery Administration

This system was established to regulate competition, ensure fair business practices, and promote renewed confidence in the economy.

_____ 9. Aid to Families with Dependent Children (AFDC)

Financial aid for families in which children have lost the support of a parent was first enacted in Illinois. The Social Security Act established a federal-state cooperative system of Aid to Dependent Children.

_____ 10. Civilian Conservation Corps

The corps was a federally funded program that paid 17- to 23-year-old men $30 a month for work on conservation projects such as state park development.

Rules and Regulations

The passage of New Deal legislation ushered in a new era of government involvement in the work world. Today agencies, commissions, and administrations regulate numerous business practices and policies. Read the hypothetical situations below and decide which government agency listed in the box would most likely be involved in the case. Write your answers on the lines provided.

Occupational Safety and Health Administration	Federal Trade Commission
National Labor Relations Board	Environmental Protection Agency
Federal Communications Commission	Food and Drug Administration
Securities and Exchange Commission	Nuclear Regulatory Commission
National Highway Traffic Safety Administration	Federal Reserve Board
Consumer Product Safety Commission	Antitrust Division of Justice Dept.

_____ 1. If four major phone companies decided to work together to install a new Internet cable that would be available through no other company, they would likely have to talk with which government commission first?

_____ 2. Which government administration might tell a canned foods company to its products' ingredients?

_____ 3. A foundry on the Ohio River might be told not to dump waste into the river by which agency?

_____ 4. Which administration might give states extra money for keeping the speed limit at 55 mph for highway driving?

_____ 5. A car seat maker might be ordered to recall a car seat model that does not work correctly by which government commission?

_____ 6. A nuclear power company might not be allowed to build a plant within 100 hundred miles from an area where people live according to the rules of which commission?

_____ 7. Brochures that talk about fair competition might be given to private businesses by which government commission?

_____ 8. Government bonds can be bought from banks by which board?

_____ 9. A company could get in trouble for hiring only white men by which government board?

_____ 10. If a major office supply company wished to buy out another major office supply company, threatening to put smaller office supply companies out of business, which government department could forbid the buyout?

_____ 11. If a new, highly successful biotech firm wanted the okay to sell stock, they would talk to which commission?

_____ 12. A chemical manufacturing company might be told to keep a safety manual on a shelf in each of its 20 laboratories by which government administration?

Putting It in Perspective

Franklin D. Roosevelt was president through two of the most difficult periods in American history—the Great Depression and World War II. Balancing domestic and international concerns was challenging for the president, and losing farms and jobs at home and sons and brothers overseas was not easy for the general public. Try to put New Deal legislation in perspective by determining the dates of the following historical happenings by using your knowledge of key words to locate events in your history book or an encyclopedia. Then place them on the proper location on the time line. The first one (letter A) has already been done for you.

A. World War II begins as a conflict between Germany and an Anglo-French coalition.
B. Franklin D. Roosevelt dies in Warm Springs, Georgia.
C. The Social Security Act is enacted.
D. The stock market crashes.
E. Franklin D. Roosevelt gives his inaugural speech.
F. The Japanese attack Pearl Harbor.
G. Einstein and others inform the president of the capability of building an atom bomb.
H. Germany surrenders.
 I. A national minimum wage is enacted.
J. New Deal legislation begins with the "First Hundred Days."
K. The United States enters World War II.
L. Hiroshima and Nagasaki are bombed by the United States.
M. Churchill and Roosevelt sign the Atlantic Charter supporting universal human rights.
N. Japan surrenders.

Oct. 29, 1929	March 4, 1933	March 9-June 16, 1933	August 14, 1935	June 28, 1938	August 2, 1939	Sept. 3, 1939 A

August 14, 1941	Dec. 7, 1941	Dec. 8, 1941	April 12, 1945	May 7, 1945	August 6, August 9, 1945	August 15, 1945

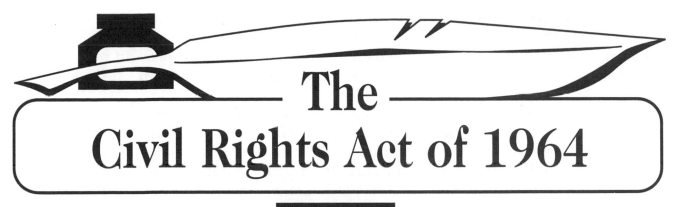

The Civil Rights Act of 1964

In theory, the Reconstruction amendments of the 1860s abolished slavery and guaranteed to all U.S. citizens equal rights and privileges referred to in the Constitution, equal protection of the laws, and the assurance that the right to vote would not be denied "on account of race, color, or previous condition of servitude." In practice, minorities continue to fight for equality of citizenship in legal and social arenas throughout America today.

Many laws and practices after the abolition of slavery segregated blacks and whites deliberately. Black codes in the South that prevented former slaves from owning property, voting, or bearing arms were struck down by the Fourteenth and Fifteenth Amendments. However, in 1896 the Supreme Court voted to allow segregation in restaurants, schools, and other public places when it ruled in the *Plessy* v. *Ferguson* case that separate facilities could legally be considered equal facilities. This ruling virtually endorsed the ongoing social, economic, and political discrimination against minorities in America.

With each injustice, a growing civil rights movement gained momentum. The *Plessy* v. *Ferguson* decision prompted the creation of black organizations, such as the National Association for the Advancement of Colored People and the National Urban League that challenged segregation in Southern courts. The Great Depression practice of hiring only white salesmen in white-owned, black-district stores united blacks in boycotts of the businesses under the slogan, "Don't Buy Where You Can't Work." Injustices suffered by soldiers during World War II encouraged black newspaper editors to demand an end to discrimination in the military. And the emergence of a "Harlem Renaissance" in the North, where black urban communities sprang up in response to industrial job openings created by both world wars, served to integrate the races who could all appreciate the poems of Langston Hughes and the music of Louis Armstrong and Jelly Roll Morton.

In 1957 the Supreme Court reversed itself, asserting that separate was inherently unequal in the landmark *Brown* v. *Board of Education* case. The South resisted. President Eisenhower had to send federal troops to Little Rock,

Arkansas, so that nine black high school students could get past the front door of Central High School where they were legally allowed to attend. In 1962 Governor Ross Barnett defied a court order and attempted to prevent a young black man, James Meredith, from enrolling in the University of Mississippi.

Finally on July 2, 1964, the eighty-eighth Congress of the United States passed the Civil Rights Act of 1964 as a tribute to John F. Kennedy's memory and against the wishes of many Southern legislators. The resulting legal rulings and commissions have not erased discrimination but have defined for all United States citizens what is meant by true economic, social, and political equality.

In this lesson students read and answer questions about a letter from a grandfather to his grandchildren in which he speaks of his first-hand knowledge of the movement that led to the Civil Rights Act of 1964 and the changes that accompanied its passage. Through student activities and extensions they examine each title of the act individually, consider the struggle for equality experienced by immigrants, compare and contrast several civil rights groups and leaders, and discuss recent civil rights cases.

Teaching Activities

Grandpa's Wisdom

Students discuss the student reading with fellow classmates.

The Jury Is Still Out

Students examine the Civil Rights Act of 1964 title by title and decide whether the scenarios that follow violate any part of the act.

A Newcomer's Welcome

Students decide whether past and present U.S. immigration policies are discriminatory.

Alphabet Soup

Students learn the differences in the philosophies and practices of the NAACP, the SNCC, the SCLC, and other civil rights organizations of the sixties and today.

Extensions

1. Assign research and reporting on the lives and accomplishments of civil rights activists including Thurgood Marshall, Martin Luther King, Jr., Stokely Carmichael, Robert Moses, Ella Baker, W. E. B. Du Bois, Philip Randolph, and Rosa Parks.

2. Locate and discuss examples of the historical changes in attitude toward minorities in the United States as demonstrated in novels, movies, textbooks, and news accounts from different eras in American history.

3. Research the history of children's rights in America (child labor and child abuse laws).

4. Research and report on the treatment of minorities in other places and eras in history. Which modern countries come closest to providing all citizens with equal rights and protections under their laws and constitutions? Which modern countries continue to discriminate not only in practice but under the law?

5. Locate periodical articles pertaining to recent civil rights cases in the court system. Discuss the articles, conduct debates, and/or draw political cartoons that express individual student opinions about the issues raised by each case.

6. Discuss situations in which civil rights are limited, for example, in prisons, in schools, and during times of national emergency. Should civil rights ever be limited? If so, how should the line be drawn defining when and upon whom limits should be placed?

7. Discuss variant cultural and political interpretations of human rights. China's leader, for example, contends that food and shelter are human rights and that individual civil injustices are sometimes necessary to assure those rights. Can there be a single definition of human rights such as that defined in the United Nation's *Universal Declaration of Human Rights,* or do cultures differ too much to agree on a single definition?

GRANDPA'S WISDOM

Dear Children, Grandchildren, and Great-Grandchildren,

As I approach my one hundredth year in this world, I am acutely aware that I may not be around for too terribly many more birthday celebrations, and so I write you now these extraordinary stories of my life so that they will not have been experienced in vain.

I was born at the very turn of the century, in the month of May, the year 1900. The Plessy v. Ferguson case of four years earlier, which refused to stop segregation policies, weighed heavily on the minds of my mother and father. They had struggled so hard for economic equality—pouring sweat and endless hours into the creation of a very successful mom-and-pop grocery store in an all-black neighborhood on the north side of Chicago—only to find that social equality was legally out of their reach. Railroad cars, restaurants, and movie theaters—even bathrooms and drinking fountains—throughout the city displayed "Whites Only" signs, and the Supreme Court of the United States declared there was nothing an African American or Chinese or Native American could do about it.

Perhaps it was the frustration that my parents felt in being legally unable to challenge such discriminatory practices that prompted me to apply for my first job with the National Association for the Advancement of Colored People. The NAACP was created in 1909 after whites in Springfield tried to remove blacks from the neighborhood. The event made big news then—especially in Illinois—and I promised myself at nine years of age that I would one day join that group of people who committed to a campaign against lynching. You could get jobs and meet really important people back then just by being a pretty good talker, I guess, because I somehow landed that NAACP job in 1920 proofreading articles for the organization's magazine, The Crisis, edited by W.E.B. Du Bois.

Well, the proofreader's desk proved to be the perfect place for me because I not only got to meet Du Bois himself many times and Thurgood Marshall to boot (back when he was a young lawyer with not a dream of being one day appointed to the United States Supreme Court), but I also got advance notice of every civil rights action or violation that affected the nation for the next 50 years.

The world wars provided numerous stories for our magazine, which was dedicated to condemning practices of segregation until they were no more. Du Bois published stories of black soldiers in World War I segregated in all-black barracks and denied medals and military promotions. The Crisis told how the urbanization of blacks that occurred as Southern blacks migrated north to take industrial jobs created by the war led to unified black communities with increasing political clout. By the days of the next world war, Du Bois, along with black newspaper editors nationwide, was insisting minorities in this war would be treated as equals. When Philip Randolph threatened a march on Washington, Franklin D. Roosevelt issued an executive order that required all defense contractors to hire blacks and whites on an equal basis, and by the end of the second world war, American armed forces were legally desegregated.

The NAACP's Legal Defense Fund won many cases in the 1950s, the greatest of which was the 1954 Brown v. Board of Education decision that declared that separate schools were inherently unequal. The original goal of the organization was being realized in the courts. A party for Thurgood Marshall after that Supreme Court decision is an event I will never forget, but changing laws and changing public opinions are two different things, as we were to discover.

School desegregation happened very slowly, and public businesses continued to prohibit blacks or limit them to separate seating or sections of the premises. When Rosa Parks was arrested in December of 1955 for not surrendering her seat to a white person on a city bus in Montgomery, Alabama, I knew my dedication to the civil rights movement had to go beyond my proofreading desk at The Crisis. I was 55 years old and ready to scale down to part-time work anyway, so I joined in the marches of Martin Luther King, Jr.'s, Southern Christian Leadership Conference. I think your grandmother wanted to protest that I was too old to go gallivanting around the country, but she understood. Already I was a grandfather and I did not desire to see another generation of minorities treated as inferior citizens of this nation.

The goal of the Southern Christian Leadership Conference was to stir Washington to action. The tactic of the SCLC was this: create social and political unrest peacefully by eating at "Whites Only" tables in restaurants, riding in the front seats of buses, walking in protest marches throughout the South, and attending demonstrations where Martin Luther King, Jr., and others would speak to the cheers (and sometimes jeers) of large crowds.

Just like you've read about in your school books, I was spat upon, yelled at, arrested, and jailed. A mob beat a group of us protesting in Montgomery, Alabama, and Police Commissioner Eugene Connor told his officers to turn dogs and firehoses on us in Birmingham. But each violent outburst made the nightly news and brought us one step closer to the passage of the Civil Rights Act of 1964.

The 200,000-people March on Washington in August of 1963 and Mr. King's "I Have a Dream" speech are likely what most encouraged President Kennedy to propose new civil rights legislation, and his deplorable assassination in November of the same year prompted President Johnson to urge Congress to accept the Civil Rights Act on July 2, 1964.

I returned to Chicago and to your grandmother where we waited to see just how the act would change the lives of our children and grandchildren and great-grandchildren. Segregation was outlawed and we were legally allowed to sit at any lunch counter in the city, but the feeling that whites were staring as though we didn't belong there never left your grandmother or me. I fear that my offspring feel the same way when walking through all-white neighborhoods today. Minorities now have the vote. We now have legal recourse when discriminated against on the job or in the housing market. But too many of our new generation are raised in poverty and slums, wind up in prison or on drugs or murdered, and the battle still seems to be uphill.

Just before his assassination, Martin Luther King, Jr., had turned his attention to economic issues, organizing what he called the Poor People's Campaign. His new goal proved even more difficult than his fight to end segregation because the problems of poverty cannot be traced to specific laws that can be targeted for change. Affirmative Action policies attempt to address silent discriminatory practices, but no one likes hiring quotas. Welfare reform is aimed only at reducing government spending, not at recreating the system so that financial public assistance programs can be realistically eliminated.

The fight for equality has moved beyond the color battle it started out to be. I urge you, my children, grandchildren, and great-grandchildren, to demand equal rights and privileges under the Constitution, equal protection under the law, and equal political clout for all U.S. citizens regardless of economic status. Fight for the equality of the minimum wage earner and the migrant farmer. Fight for the equality of the factory worker and the schoolteacher. Refuse to buy into the Cinderella dream that anyone can grow up to be Michael Jordan or Bill Gates. The rich are rich because the poor are poor. Peacefully appeal to the moral convictions we all hold in our hearts as Mr. King did in demanding equality for all, regardless of color, sex, religious beliefs, ethnic background, personal living practices, or size of pocketbook.

I wish you a long and meaningful journey in life in the century to come. I love you all.

Grandpa Jimmy

Grandpa's Wisdom

On your own paper, answer the following questions based on the student reading.

1. Some historians contend that the civil rights movement ended with the death of Martin Luther King, Jr., while others suggest that the march will go on until true equality for minorities is realized. What evidence can you cite that ethnic and religious minorities, women, homosexuals, immigrants, and other "outsiders" have not yet realized equality? Is there evidence that the civil rights movement continues today?

2. Grandpa Jimmy lived an extraordinarily full 100 years. How might the experiences of the average black man have differed from the experiences he attested to in the 1920s? The 1950s? The 1990s? What may have been the experiences of the average black woman during those years? What about the experiences of a white woman?

3. Imagine the year is 2100 and a grandfather is about to write a letter to his grandchildren about significant social events of his lifetime. What will he write about? What will be the moral, social, political, and economic issues of the next 100 years? Will all citizens of America enjoy true equality in 100 years? Will there be a struggle before that happens? Will we live under the same constitution and economic system of capitalism? Will we continue to live in a democracy? How will technological advances change our lives (consider gene therapy, cloning, robots, and computers)? Will we have mended our ailing environment in 100 years?

4. Before the Civil Rights Act of 1964, state and city laws and ordinances worked around existing laws to create unfair conditions under which minorities lived. For example, although the Fifteenth Amendment made it illegal to bar a person from voting "on account of race, color, or previous condition of servitude," some states did prevent minorities from voting by requiring voters to own property, pass written tests, or have a grandfather who had voted in a previous election. In what ways do states, cities, or institutions continue to treat minorities unjustly in spite of civil rights laws?

5. The struggle for the passage of the Civil Rights Act began long before the 1950s, according to Grandpa Jimmy's account. Blacks had been fighting for equality since the abolition of slavery and the ratification of the Thirteenth Amendment. Outline Grandpa Jimmy's account of the movement beginning with the *Plessy* v. *Ferguson* case of 1896.

6. Do you agree with Grandpa Jimmy that the civil rights movement of today must focus on equality for low- and middle-class people? Do wealthy citizens carry more political clout? How can a democracy ensure that the voices of all are heard?

The Jury Is Still Out

On July 2, 1964, the eighty-eighth Congress announced an act

"To enforce the constitutional right to vote, to confer jurisdiction upon the district courts of the United States to provide injunctive relief against discrimination in public accommodations, to authorize the Attorney General to institute suits to protect constitutional rights in public education, to extend the Commission on Civil Rights, to prevent discrimination in federally assisted programs, to establish a Commission on Equal Employment Opportunity, and for other purposes."

Study the following summaries of the 11 titles that constitute the Civil Rights Act of 1964. Then decide whether the scenarios that follow the summaries violate any part of the act. Be certain to justify your opinion with facts or logic.

Title I—Voting Rights

This title assures all qualified citizens be permitted to vote in federal elections by demanding that a single standard be used to determine the eligibility of all voters, that an "error or omission on any record or paper relating to any application" not disqualify a person from voting, and that qualifying tests follow strict rules. (Note: Amendments to the Voting Rights Act of 1965 later banned the use of any voter qualification tests.)

The title provides for the submission of grievance to the courts should a "pattern or practice of discrimination" be found.

Title II—Injunctive Relief Against Discrimination in Places of Public Accommodation

This title insures that "all persons shall be entitled to the full and equal enjoyment of the goods, services, facilities, privileges, advantages, and accommodations" of such public places as restaurants, hotels, theaters, concert halls, sports arenas, and the like. It deems it illegal to "intimidate, threaten, or coerce" another in an attempt to withhold such rights and privileges. The title specifically states that its requirements do not apply to private organizations.

The title outlines the specific proceedings an attorney general or other person can follow in trying cases pertaining to this title.

Title III—Desegregation of Public Facilities

This title outlines the attorney general's role in "furthering the orderly progress of desegregation in public facilities." It provides that the attorney general can represent people unable to represent themselves for reasons of safety, a threat to employment, or a lack of funds.

Title IV—Desegregation of Public Education

According to this title, *desegregation* refers to the "assignment of students to public schools and within such schools without regard to their race, color, religion, or national origin." It does not mean "the assignment of students to public schools in order to overcome racial imbalances."

This title creates the position of commissioner of education who is to research and report to the president and to congress "concerning the lack of availability of equal education opportunities" for minorities at all levels of public education. The commissioner is also authorized within this act to provide grants, training, and technical support in the implementation of desegregation of education.

The attorney general is given permission to press suits of discrimination based on the title.

Title V—Commission on Civil Rights

This title establishes a Civil Rights Commission and describes its duties and methods of operation. In general, the commission's job is to:

a. "investigate allegations . . . that certain citizens of the United States are being deprived of their right to vote . . . by reason of their color, race, religion, or national origin,"
b. "appraise laws and policies of the federal government with respect to denials of equal protection of the laws under the Constitution,"
c. act as a clearinghouse of information on discrimination, and
d. submit periodic reports to Congress and the president and publish their methods and procedures in the federal register.

Title VI—Nondiscrimination in Federally Assisted Programs

This title ensures that any "program or activity receiving federal financial assistance" will not discriminate, exclude from participation, or deny benefits on the grounds of "race, color, or national origin."

Title VII—Equal Employment Opportunity

This title demands that a person not be discriminated against in the work world on the basis of "race, color, religion, sex, or national origin" in respect to hiring and firing procedures, compensation scales, classification of employees, or any other "terms, conditions, or privileges of employment."

Indian reservations, "employment of aliens outside any state," and certain religious employers are exempt. For example, a Catholic church can refuse to hire a Methodist pastor, and an employer on an Indian reservation can insist on hiring an Native American.

It is further stated that "nothing contained in this title shall be interpreted to require any employer, employment agency . . . to grant preferential treatment to any individual or to any group because of race, color, religion, sex, or national origin."

Finally, this title establishes an Equal Employment Opportunity Commission whose five members' duties include studying policy compliance issues, investigating possible violations, referring certain matters to the attorney general, and making periodic reports to the congress and president.

Title VIII—Registration and Voting Statistics

This act states that the "Secretary of Commerce shall promptly conduct a survey to compile registration and voting statistics" to, among other things, determine the percentage of registered and voting citizens of various races, colors, and national origins. The act allows that individuals have the right not to report such information should they choose not to.

Title IX—Intervention and Procedures after Removal in Civil Rights Cases

Under this title, the attorney general is given the authority to intervene in discrimination cases of "general public interest."

Title X—Establishment of Community Relations Service

This service, which is to serve under the Department of Commerce, shall "provide assistance to communities and persons therein in resolving disputes, disagreements, or difficulties relating to discriminatory practices based on race, color, or national origin . . . ." The Community Relations Service is directed to cooperate with appropriate "state, local, public, or private agencies."

Title XI—Miscellaneous

This title ensures a trial by jury for anyone accused of contempt of any of the other titles of the act and spells out the rights of the accused as well as stating a number of ways in which the act is not to be construed in practice.

Case Scenarios

Decide whether each of the following cases violates the Civil Rights Act of 1964. If you believe a violation exists, state the title being violated. In each case justify your conclusion with facts and/or logic.

1. A public elementary school sponsors a boys' soccer team but offers no sports program to girls.
   YOUR DECISION:

2. A public high school will not allow the formation of a school-sponsored Christian club although it does sponsor a math club, a French club, and a Hispanic-Americans club.
   YOUR DECISION:

3. A television station hires a female news coanchor to complement the male anchor who already works at the station.
   YOUR DECISION:

4. A homeless 32-year-old male is not permitted to register to vote because he has no permanent address.
YOUR DECISION:

5. The Commission on Civil Rights neglects to mention in the federal register a policy of requiring witnesses to appear within 20 minutes of a prearranged time scheduled and reported to the witness prior to the hearing. When a certain witness arrives at the hearing 30 minutes late, he is not allowed to speak.
YOUR DECISION:

6. A certain church reserves special pews for nonmembers.
YOUR DECISION:

7. A public sports bar sponsors a "Boys Night Out" on Wednesday nights when women are not permitted and a "Girls Night Out" on Thursday nights when they permit only women.
YOUR DECISION:

8. The owner of an Indian restaurant in an Indian district of a large city casts looks of scorn to nonIndian customers but does not refuse to serve them or directly ask them to leave.
YOUR DECISION:

9. A state college library contains hundreds of books that recount the lives of white heroes from American history but does not contain a single book on minority American heroes.
YOUR DECISION:

10. A Fortune 500 company has no minority employees in upper management positions.
YOUR DECISION:

11. The entire population of a public school in downtown Austin, Texas, is Hispanic, as is the population of the community in which the students live.
YOUR DECISION:

A Newcomer's Welcome

The United States is a nation of immigrants. Between 1880 and 1920 alone, 23 million immigrants arrived on our shores. Recent immigrants and their descendants are predicted to contribute as much as 90% of our nation's growth in the next century. Fear of diversity, attempts at population control, and other just and unjust motives have prompted periodic legislation addressing issues of immigration in the United States. Decide which of the following United States immigration policies are (were) discriminatory in nature and list them in the Discriminatory Policies Column. List all others in the Nondiscriminatory Policies Column. Be prepared to justify your decisions.

Discriminatory Policies	Nondiscriminatory Policies
_____	_____
_____	_____
_____	_____
_____	_____
_____	_____
_____	_____
_____	_____
_____	_____

The Burlingame Treaty of 1868
This document gave Chinese the right to immigrate to America.

1875 Congressional Ban
During the seventeenth century, immigration to the New World was encouraged by colonists who actively recruited northern and western Europeans to join them in America. By the mid 1880s America had absorbed so many immigrants from all over Europe that native-born Americans began to fear the diversity of the newcomers, and Congress enacted a ban on convicts, alcoholics, illiterates, Communists, the insane, and others.

The Fourteenth Amendment (1868)
Ratified not without a fight following the Civil War, this amendment ensures that "all persons born or naturalized in the United States, and subject to the jurisdiction thereof are citizens of the United States" whose citizenship rights cannot be abridged.

The Chinese Exclusion Acts of 1882, 1892, and 1902
Economic competition among the many Chinese who came to the West Coast

after the discovery of gold and during the construction of the Central Pacific Railroad and native-born whites led to these three acts that prohibited Chinese immigration to the United States.

Immigration and Nationality Act of 1924
This act set up a "national origins" policy reducing the number of immigrants the United States would accept from southern and eastern European countries and limited the total number of immigrants that would be admitted annually.

Executive Order 9066 (February 19, 1942)
Japanese people who began immigrating to the United States in 1882 were—60 years later—given ten days to sell their homes and possessions before being removed to relocation centers under this wartime executive order.

Amendments to the Immigration and Nationality Act (1965)
Under fire from the civil rights movement of the period, these amendments repealed the "national origins" provision of the Immigration and Nationality Act.

The Refugee Act of 1980
This act provided for the admission of refugees to the United States.

The Immigration Reform and Control Act of 1986
This act was constructed to deal with illegal immigration. In addition to setting up penalties for employers who knowingly employ illegal aliens and legalizing a large number of illegal aliens already in the country, the act deems family relationships and needed skills as determinants of who will be admitted to the United States.

Proposition 187 (1994)
This proposition, overwhelmingly supported by California voters, which denies all but emergency services to illegal aliens in the state, has prompted several legal cases regarding its constitutionality.

Brian Bilbray's Position (late 1990s)
United States Representative, Brian Bilbray, from Imperial Beach, California, argues that granting U.S. citizenship to children of illegal immigrants encourages Mexicans to cross the border illegally in such states as California and Texas. He contends there is nothing in the Fourteenth Amendment that guarantees citizenship to children of illegal immigrants because they are not "subject to the jurisdiction thereof" since they are not following the laws of the nation by the very fact that they are here.

Alphabet Soup

Civil rights organizations share the goal of achieving equality, but the various groups hold different specific objectives and operate using different tactics. Read the capsule description of each group listed below and then decide which of the civil activism tactics each group would likely employ. Which group(s) would you be most likely to join? Which group(s) would be the most likely to produce effects and display longevity?

Civil Activism Tactics

Peaceful Civil Disobedience
Sit-ins at restaurants
Demonstrations
Protest marches
Boycotts

Violent Activities
Acts of self-defense
Vigilante acts
Riots
Confronting police

Litigate and Legislate
Lobby congress
Prosecute discriminatory
   practices
Exercise voting power
Advocate Affirmative Action
Voter registration drives
Unite minority communities
   into socio-political bloc

Educate the Public
Distribute newsletters
Organize conventions
Endorse minority job
   training programs
Publicize discriminatory
   practices

Civil Rights Groups

1. *Congress of Racial Equality (CORE)*
   CORE was founded by James Farmer in 1942. It advocates nonviolent, direct action that will help minorities achieve equal jobs, education, and housing. Its members hope for a society in which "race or creed will be neither asset nor handicap."

   Organization's Tactics:

2. *Southern Christian Leadership Conference (SCLC)*
   Martin Luther King, Jr.'s, civil rights group encouraged peaceful civil disobedience in an attempt to pressure congress to change laws in favor of equality for minorities. Many members were jailed in the 1960s, and Martin Luther King, Jr., was assassinated. The organization was put under FBI surveillance for opposing President Reagan's policies pertaining to Central America. Today the SCLC continues to demand equality for minorities and the poor.

   Organization's Tactics:

3. *Student Nonviolent Coordination Committee*
   This organization of 200 college students was formed in April of 1960 to organize sit-ins and support the ongoing civil rights movement. It redirected

its energies to voter registration campaigns in 1961 and cosponsored the march to Montgomery that resulted in the Voter Rights Act of 1965. In 1966 a faction of SNCC led by Stokely Carmichael took over the organization and changed goals and tactics again, now supporting violence as a means of self-defense and pushing for not just segregation, but black dignity and self-reliance.

Organization's Tactics:

4. *National Organization for Women (NOW)*
   Founded in 1966, this organization promoted the unsuccessful Equal Rights Amendment. Presently it strives to increase the number of women in public office and otherwise attempts to achieve equality for women in business, government, and all other aspects of society.

   Organization's Tactics:

5. *National Organization for the Advancement of Colored People (NAACP)*
   This organization, born in 1909 to advance the cause of equality of citizenship, claims 500,000 members today as well as a president, an executive committee, and a board of directors. The NAACP publishes a magazine entitled *The Crisis* and develops programs that address economic development, fair housing, drug abuse, violence, youth development, and prisoner rehabilitation. The organization's Legal Defense and Education Fund brings discrimination cases to court and provides scholarships for black students.

   Organization's Tactics:

6. *National Urban League*
   This organization, which claims over 100 affiliates in 34 states, works to secure equality for blacks in both social and economic situations. It attempts to educate the public on the social and economic status of blacks and to promote an understanding between the races.

   Organization's Tactics:

7. *American Indian Movement (AIM)*
   This organization's quest for U.S. governmental recognition of Native-American treaties and rights has sometimes led to confrontations with police officials that have resulted in injuries and deaths. In an attempt to pressure Congress to address its concerns, the group has occupied Alcatraz, Mt. Rushmore, a replica of the *Mayflower*, and the Bureau of Indian Affairs. It has also staged marches and protests against unjust congressional bills and unfair social and political treatment.

   Organization's Tactics:

8. *Organization of Afro-American Unity*

   Malcolm X, the founder of this organization, advocated racial separation, believing that improving black communities was a more realistic goal than complete integration into the white culture. He condoned retaliation for violence experienced by many blacks in the 1960s; at one time he even advocated the creation of a black nation.

   Organization's Tactics:

9. *American Civil Liberties Union*

   This organization was founded in 1920 to defend conscientious objectors to World War I but soon expanded its scope to the protection of the freedom of expression for all people. Defenders in the Scopes Trial and the *Brown* v. *Board of Education* suit, the organization is not afraid to defend unpopular positions. It is concerned with women's rights, censorship, and the rights of immigrants and other issues pertaining to civil liberties.

   Organization's Tactics:

10. *Black Panthers Party*

    Founded in 1966 by Bobby Seale and Huey Newton, this group advocated armed rebellion and witnessed shoot-outs and deaths in its attempt to gain minority equality. Suspected also of terrorist acts, two of the group's leaders were killed by police in 1969. Both Seale and Newton were accused of murder and eventually advocated a peaceful approach to reform.

    Organization's Tactics:

The
United Nations Charter

In the aftermath of World War II representatives from 50 nations met in San Francisco, California, determined to "save succeeding generations from the scourge of war." They signed the United Nations Charter on June 26, 1945, thereby establishing a global organization dedicated to world peace. The charter's goals, now supported by 185 member nations, include the establishment of international peace, the protection of universal human rights, the promotion of cooperation in solving world problems and expanding social progress, and the encouragement of respect for international law.

The United Nations Charter established six operating bodies including the General Assembly, the Security Council, the Economic and Social Council, the Trusteeship Council, the International Court of Justice, and the Secretariat. The charter is a flexible document that also authorizes the creation of new agencies and commissions within these operating bodies when the need arises. Additionally, the United Nations sponsors periodic global conferences that address world problems.

The achievements of the United Nations are evident. The Nobel Peace Prize has been awarded to the United Nations Children's Fund, U.N. Peace-keeping Forces, and the Office of the United Nations High Commissioner for Refugees. UNICEF currently addresses the needs of children in 138 countries. The U.N.-authored Universal Declaration of Human Rights sets the standard for the acceptable treatment of human beings worldwide.

Yet the effectiveness of the organizations operating under the United Nations' umbrella has been called into question in recent years. The United Nations Protection Force, intending to operate as peace-keepers in Bosnia and Herzegovina in 1995, found themselves being used as human shields by Bosnian Serbs in their effort to deter NATO air attacks. United Nations' humanitarian assistance personnel in Rwanda were unable to provide civil war

survivors with essential aid in the same year when their troops were deliberately attacked. In Iraq in 1997 Saddam Hussein embarrassed U.N. inspectors who wished to investigate biological warfare laboratories by turning them away at the door. United Nations' resolutions are ignored and its charter does not authorize enforcement of its decisions and recommendations.

Even while such critics accuse the U.N. of lacking power, a growing number of American citizens suspect existence of a conspiracy that intends to turn the United Nations into a tyrannical world government. Talk radio and right-wing publications are filled with assertions that U.N. troops, landed by unmarked black helicopters, will soon try to take over this country, seizing firearms from the citizenry and suspending the Constitution.

In this lesson students read a fictitious speech by a senator encouraging the United States to support the United Nations and catch up on its payment of dues to the global organization. Students then complete activities that further their understanding of the purpose of the United Nations Charter and allow them to formulate their own opinions about the effectiveness of United Nations' organizations and operations.

Teaching Activities

U.N. Dues Are Due
Choose a student to present Senator Cole's speech to fellow classmates. Then allow students to form their own opinions about the effectiveness of the United Nations and its organizations and world summits by assigning this activity based on the student reading. An answer key has been provided.

Charter of the United Classroom
Divide students into groups of four and require each group to rewrite the United Nations Preamble to create a charter for a cooperative, peaceful, and intellectually stimulating classroom. Although there is no single correct response to this activity, a plausible Classroom Charter has been provided in the answer key.

Charting the Charter
With this activity students create a chart displaying the United Nations' various branches and the agencies that operate under each branch. Although charts can take various forms, a sample chart has been provided in the answer key.

Extensions

1. Divide students into seven groups to research and report on the League of Nations, the Inter-Allied Declaration, the Atlantic Charter, the Declaration by United Nations, the Moscow and Teheran Conferences, the Dumbarton Oaks Conference, and the Yalta Conference, all of which led to the creation of the United Nations Charter.

2. The United States is currently behind on its payment of dues to the United Nations. We also donate a smaller portion of our total wealth in governmental aid to less fortunate nations than any other country in the world according to a 1997 survey conducted by volunteer groups. Research and report on America's disbursement of governmental aid. How are decisions made as to who gets assistance and for what reasons? Who decides how much will be spent on foreign aid? Is aid more likely to be dispersed to victims of natural catastrophes or of wars? To political allies or to trading partners?

3. Some people believe that the United Nations will soon become a true world government and take away freedoms in its goals to eradicate nationalism and patriotism and individualism. Using print media or the Internet, locate examples of this conspiracy theory. Are the reasonings contained logical? Is it possible that the specific accusations and fears are wrong, but the general idea is correct? Do you think, as have such idealists as Albert Einstein, that world government is necessary and inevitable? Or would world government necessarily lead to world tyranny?

4. Article 26 of the United Nations Charter makes the Security Council responsible "for the establishment of a system for the regulation of armaments." Read and discuss the book *Caging the Nuclear Genie* by ex-CIA chief, Stansfield Turner about ridding the world of nuclear weapons. Lead a class discussion on the pros and cons of a nation's possessing nuclear weapons.

5. Organize a United Nations Day. Have classes from your school represent various member countries of the United Nations. Conduct a U.N. meeting with each country's representative voicing views and voting on mock U.N. resolutions.

6. Subscribe to the *U.N. Chronicle* to transform students into "informed world citizens." Write to the United Nations Publications Subscription Office, P.O. Box 361, Birmingham, AL 35282-9363.

Speech by Senator Cole

My Fellow Senators,

The United States is over $1.3 billion behind on its payment of dues to the United Nations. On November 12 of 1997, we had the chance to vote for the expenditure of $819 million on this debt, but we declined the bill. United Nations Association of the United States, President Alvin P. Adams, has called our failure to fund the payment of our U.N. arrears "a body blow to American leadership and credibility on the world stage." I urge you to reconsider the payment of the nation's delinquent United Nations' dues.

The origins of the Charter of the United Nations can be traced to the Atlantic Charter proposed by our own President Franklin D. Roosevelt and his friend and ally, Winston Churchill. The term *United Nations* was suggested by F.D.R. himself. President Roosevelt and President Truman after him deliberated with other world leaders for over five years to forge agreement on the specifics of a document in support of world peace and cooperation. As one of the 50 original signers of the United Nations Charter, we are obligated to support it financially—even when we are offering criticism of how it works.

And the criticism has been vocal. Many of you have voiced complaints about the inefficiencies of the United Nations and its agencies. It has been argued, for example, that United Nations' resolutions and recommendations have no teeth in them. Articles 33 through 38 of the charter only authorize the Security Council to set up special investigating committees and encourage disputing parties to negotiate peace. And even though Articles 39 through 51 okay the use of both sanctions and military force when peace is threatened, the reality is the United Nations has no standing military and, therefore, must rely on availability of member countries' militias. In addition, the charter demands unanimous agreement of the Security Council's five permanent members (China, Russia, the United States, France, and Great Britain) on all decisions involving enforcement—a feat that has proved impossible most of the time.

We've also heard complaints that United Nations' organizations misuse funds or that peace-keeping operations require too much money or that the United States is unjustly overburdened with 25% of expenses. Some argue that the developing countries create a block that prevents true negotiation. Some point a finger at the 1993 Security Council tribunal investigating war crimes in Bosnia, which moves at a snail's pace, as proof of the United Nations' ineffectiveness. Others cry for reform in the world organization that will expand the powers of Japan and Germany, encourage the great powers to cooperate, and boost the enforcement capabilities of the U.N.

None of these complaints can be dismissed. Although sometimes skewed or exaggerated by United Nations' opponents to make a point, each complaint carries at least some truth. So why pay United Nations' dues? Why support a charter that seems entirely unenforceable?

Even if the United Nations accomplished nothing more than gathering world representatives once a year to discuss global issues, it would be an organization worthy of our attention and our money. If we ever hope to see a world free from war, a forum for old-fashioned dialogue between world leaders must be maintained. I do not urge you to praise the United Nations as a perfect institution. I do not ask you to agree with all United Nations' protocols and resolutions. I do not expect you to close your eyes to inefficiencies in U.N. agencies and missions. What I urge you to do is continue to finance the United Nations as you seek reforms. The United Nations is an essential forum for the encouragement of world peace and cooperation, and for the half century since it was brought into being, it has been successful in "saving succeeding generations from the scourge of war." Let it go on doing so!

Sincerely,

William J. Cole

Senator William Cole

U.N. Dues Are Due

Senator Cole mentioned several common complaints about the operations of the United Nations today. Was the United Nations Charter set up in such a way that the organization can be effective in promoting global cooperation and establishing world peace? Answer the following opinion questions on your own paper.

1. The Security Council—a 15-member U.N. body—responsible for making decisions about peace and security includes five permanent seats (the United States, Russia, Great Britain, China, and France), any of which can veto substantial decisions such as accepting a new member nation or calling for sanctions or military action against a country that is threatening world peace. This veto power was used heavily by the USSR during the cold war years, crippling the United Nation's ability to achieve peace in the world. Is this "great power unanimity" rule a good rule to maintain? Why or why not? Should there be five permanent seats on the Security Council? Why or why not? Are there other countries who should also have a permanent seat? If so, which countries? Why?

2. According to a 1995 United Nations' dues schedule, only 14 of the 185 member nations of the U.N. pay more than 1% of the operating budget which covers the expenses of ongoing activities under the charter. The United States pays the highest dues at 25% of the budget. Next is Japan which pays 14%. Only seven other countries provide more than 2% of the budget each. Why do you think the United States is charged so much for its membership in the United Nations? Is it fair to expect so much money from the United States?

3. Because the United Nations is intended to be a world organization and not a world government, the United Nations Charter did not provide any means of enforcement of resolutions adopted by the General Assembly—the U.N. organ that operates as the main forum for discussion among the representatives of all member nations. Should General Assembly resolutions be enforceable? Why or why not?

4. Although the U.N.'s International Court of Justice decisions could be enforced by the Security Council under the principles of the charter, such a decision never has been made. Should the Security Council enforce International Court of Justice decisions?

Discuss with your classmates magazine and newspaper articles and radio and television news stories that refer to United Nations operations. Then answer the questions below based on the criticisms of the U.N. mentioned in Senator Cole's speech.

A. Is the United Nations dragging its feet on convicting war criminals from the war in Bosnia?
B. Are U.N. peace-keeping forces effective in protecting civilians? Initiating negotiations for peace? Providing humanitarian relief to civilians affected by war?
C. Are U.N. resolutions and recommendations ignored by world leaders?

Charter of the United Classroom

The Preamble, written by American poet Archibald MacLeish, is presented in its entirety below, and a form for your own preamble is provided on the next page. Elect a secretary to record your group's responses on the form provided.

Preamble to the Charter of the United Nations

WE THE PEOPLE OF THE UNITED NATIONS DETERMINED

- to save succeeding generations from the scourge of war, which twice in our lifetimes has brought untold sorrow to mankind, and

- to reaffirm faith in fundamental human rights, in the dignity and worth of the human person, in the equal rights of men and women and of nations large and small, and

- to establish conditions under which justice and respect for the obligations arising from treaties and other sources of international law can be maintained, and

- to promote social progress and better standards of life in larger freedom,

AND FOR THESE ENDS

- to practice tolerance and to live together in peace with one another as good neighbors, and

- to unite our strength to maintain international peace and security, and

- to ensure, by the acceptance of principles and the institutions of methods, that armed force shall not be used, save the common interest, and

- to employ international machinery for the promotion of economic and social advancement of all peoples,

HAVE RESOLVED TO COMBINE OUR EFFORTS TO ACCOMPLISH THESE AIMS.

Accordingly, our respective Governments, through representatives assembled in the city of San Francisco, who have exhibited their full powers found to be in good and due form, have agreed to present the Charter of the United Nations and do hereby establish an international organization to be known as the United Nations.

Signed on 26 June 1945, San Francisco

Charter of the United Classroom

With the other members of your group, rewrite the United Nations Preamble bullet by bullet to create a charter for a peacefully run classroom. Select a secretary from your group to write your preamble.

We the students of _____ class are determined

*

*

*

*

And will attempt

*

*

*

*

We hope to accomplish these aims with the agreement of all students and the help and support of our teachers and administrators.

Charting the Charter

The United Nations Charter established only six operating bodies, but it authorized a working relationship with numerous other pre-existing and later-added independent agencies that have their own membership and administration but operate under the U.N. umbrella. Below are listed the six principal organs of the United Nations and many of the related agencies with a brief description of each and a statement about which body the agency functions under. On your own paper, create a chart reflecting which agency operates under which principal United Nations' body. Be certain your chart also reflects the fact that the General Assembly supervises the work of the other five principal bodies.

United Nations Principal Bodies Established by the Charter

General Assembly

This assembly consists of representatives from each member nation who meet annually, and on special occasions to discuss and make recommendations about political, social, and economic issues that affect the world. Although it oversees the operations of the other principal bodies, it is not the most powerful because the charter afforded it no means of enforcing its resolutions.

Security Council

This 15-member body includes five permanent seats and nine general assembly positions which are two-year terms. The council is responsible for making decisions about peace and security. Under Chapter VII of the charter, the Security Council is the only body that can enforce its decisions through sanctions or even military action. Any of the five permanent seats can veto a decision. This rule has led to much controversy, and the 1950 United for Peace resolution now ensures the assembly can continue to discuss a vetoed issue.

Economic and Security Council

This 54-member panel coordinates the activities of numerous independently financed and administered organizations as it addresses economic, social, cultural, educational, and health matters.

International Court of Justice

Comprised of nine judges elected by a majority vote of the Security Council and the General Assembly, this court decides legal cases between nations. Article 94 of the charter spells out the specifics of how cases are brought to the court. Although court decisions can be enforced by the Security Council in principle, only 43 nations have signed agreements to accept automatic compliance with World Court decisions. President Reagan withdrew the United States from its long-standing agreement, and numerous countries have ignored the courts as did Iran in 1980 when it was instructed to release 53 American hostages.

Secretariat

Headed by the Secretary General who acts as the United Nations' spokesperson, this body administers U.N. operations and comprises a staff of civil servants who work for the betterment of citizens of the entire world and who pledge "not to seek or accept instructions in regard to the performance of (their) duties from any Government or other authority external to the Organization." Under Article 100 of the charter, United Nations Secretariat staff operate under the principle of loyalty to the world rather than to any given nation.

Trusteeship Council

Given control of nonself-governing countries, this council suspended operations in 1994 when Palau became self-governing.

Agencies Operating Under the U.N. Umbrella

United Nations Educational, Scientific, and Cultural Organization (UNESCO)

Operating under the Economic and Social Council, this organization works to promote peace by focusing on human science issues. The group encourages education for all, the free flow of information, and the protection of cultural heritage.

United Nations Children's Fund (UNICEF)

Operating under the General Assembly, this organization provides aid to children and mothers in 138 developing countries.

World Trade Organization (WTO)

Operating under the Economic and social council, this organization oversees trade agreements and treaties and settles trade disputes.

International Labor Organization (ILO)

Operating under the Economic and Social Council, this group works to improve labor conditions and standards of living worldwide.

International Atomic Energy Agency (IAEA)

Operating under the General Assembly, this agency promotes the peaceful use of atomic energy.

United Nations High Commissioner for Refugees (UNHCR)

Operating under the General Assembly, this commission provides assistance to refugees worldwide.

United Nations Truce Supervisory Organization in Palestine (UNTSO)

Operating under the Security Council, this was one of the first groups of peace-keepers established under the United Nations Charter and is still functional today.

The
Earth Summit Agreements

Background

The majority of significant historical documents is political in nature: letters declaring independence, acts defining civil liberties, and constitutions establishing parliamentary procedures. It is impossible to overemphasize the importance of Hammurabi's Code of Law as a precedent for the codification of citizen rights and responsibilities or to deny the present-day significance of the United States Constitution that continues to serve as the fundamental law of the land for the world's wealthiest nation. Yet significant documents of the future may well be bigger than politics.

In 1840 a German biochemist named Justus von Liebig proposed to the scientific community what is now accepted as the basic principle of ecology. The Law of Minimum maintains that the population growth of any living organism is limited by environmental factors including the finiteness of natural resources. George Perkins Marsh expanded on von Liebig's thoughts 25 years later in his 1864 book, *Man and Nature*, which demonstrated that agricultural practices and other human activities negatively affect the earth causing deforestation, animal extinctions, and changes in weather patterns.

The United States was one of the first countries to heed the message of these men that the preservation of land, water, and atmosphere are essential to the continued presence of human beings on earth. John Muir founded the Sierra Club in 1892; Theodore Roosevelt expanded the nation's park system and protected forests, wetlands, and prairies in the early 1890s; Franklin Roosevelt put men to work during the Great Depression maintaining and improving wildlife areas as members of the Civilian Conservation Corps, and numerous acts have been passed and governmental agencies established in an attempt to control pollution and set environmental standards for this country.

When the United Nations sponsored the first international meeting to discuss environmental issues in 1972, the United States took a leading role. Then one of only 11 countries to have an environmental agency, the United States now cooperates with nations worldwide on pollution, global warming, population growth, and other environmental concerns. In 1991 NASA announced its Mission to Planet Earth program that links satellites from around the globe to observe how human policies and natural occurrences affect the land, ocean, and atmosphere. The findings of this and other researches have led to international documents that go beyond the politics of any single nation.

In June of 1992 Rio de Janeiro, Brazil, played host to history's largest gathering of world leaders when the United Nations-sponsored Earth Summit was held there. The conference produced two major treaties and an initiative entitled "Local Agenda 21" which outlined global policies of "sustainable development"— ways in which to raise the standard of living for all of the world's people without destroying the global environment. Since then an Earth Summit 11 conference has brought together over 100 presidents and prime ministers in New York, and more than 100 countries have established commissions to recommend sustainable development strategies. Still, the numerous action plans, agendas, conferences, and commissions have insufficiently addressed the formidable problems of global warming, ocean pollution, habitat destruction, and species extinction.

In this lesson, students examine three significant documents that came out of 1992's Earth Summit in Rio de Janeiro as they read a lecture review. Activities that follow focus on the student reading and a document signed by over 1,500 members of the world's scientific community entitled *Warning to Humanity*.

Teaching Activities

Global Agreements

Students consider discussion questions based on the student reading.

Forestalling Disaster

Students learn why over 1,500 of the world's most respected scientists are suggesting that "human beings and the natural world are on a collision course" as they investigate the "critical stresses" the environment is currently suffering according to the Union of Concerned Scientists' *Warning to Humanity*.

1. In addition to the problems associated with getting governments from various political ideologies to cooperate, the slow pace of success in addressing issues of environmental concern can also be ascribed to the complexity of the issues. Give your students a crash course in ecology by requiring them to locate in a dictionary, encyclopedia, or science book the definitions of *global warming, ozone layer, greenhouse effect, greenhouse gas emissions, precipitation, desertification, environment, ecosystem, ecology, rain forest, sustainable development,* and *population carrying capacity.*

2. Study the history of the environmental movement by assigning reports on Justus von Liebig, James Lovelock, George Perkins Marsh, Ralph Waldo Emerson, Henry David Thoreau, Rachel Carson, the transcendentalists, Theodore Roosevelt, Gifford Pinchot, John Muir, the history of Greenpeace and other grassroots environmental organizations, worldwide environmental political parties called Green Parties, the history of the passage of the Clean Water Act, the Clean Air Act, the Endangered Species Act, the Resource Conservation and Recovery Act, as well as the establishment of the Environmental Protection Agency and Earth Day celebrations.

3. Assign individual students the writing of a single, binding document that all nations of the world could sign that would ensure the survival of the planet and human beings on it.

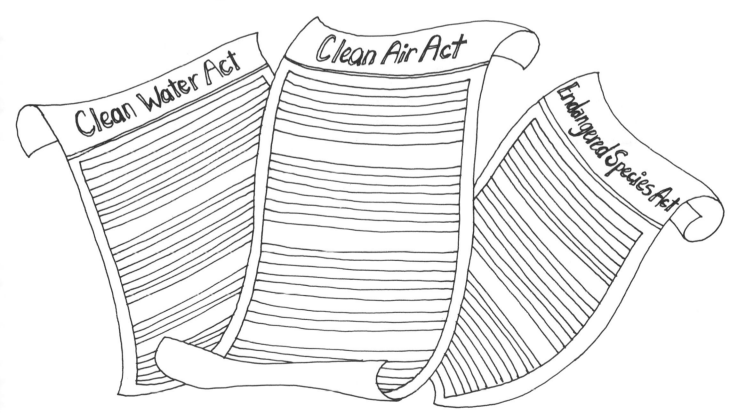

A COLUMBIA CITY CHRONICLE
LECTURE REVIEW

Last night Nobel Laureate prize-winning biochemist John Jones addressed over 57 nongovernmental organizations including environmental groups, social groups, and voluntary and professional grassroots organizations concerned with the state of the globe with his lecture entitled "A Single, Legally Binding Document." Over 650 people crowded the hall to hear Dr. Jones describe the treaties and initiatives set forth at the first Earth Summit held in Rio de Janeiro several years ago, and the progress—and lack thereof—nations have made in implementing the agreements.

Dr. Jones, who speaks to nongovernmental organizations, school children, and political leaders throughout the nation about the ineffectiveness of the summit and the need for a new approach to establishing global policies of sustaining development, always begins with the same line, "1992 marked the year of promise." Although numerous other conferences and conventions on endangered species, climate change, pollution control, and safe drinking water had been held worldwide during Dr. Jones' 37 years at the Manhattan Academy of Life Sciences, the 1992 Earth Summit was to address the entire set of problems with an audience of presidents and prime ministers.

According to Jones, a 400-page compilation of 2,000 recommendations entitled *Local Agenda 21* initiated a course of action for the 150+ nations that attended the 1992 conference. It stipulated that economic, social, and environmental factors would be taken into consideration by individual national councils that would be formed under the initiative when they gathered to formulate ways of improving the quality of life for human beings *without* destroying the global environment. Three treaties were proposed to specify the terms of the initiative. According to Dr. Jones, *Local Agenda 21* had the potential for change.

Then the debates began. Although 150 nations signed the Climate Control Treaty, its phrasing only constituted the most general agreement that greenhouse gas emissions must be reduced. Proposals for emissions reductions varied from country to country with national goals ranging from 85% of 1990 level emissions by 2010 to levels equal to that of 1990 by the year 2015. Regardless of the goals, the year 1996 witnessed a global all-time high in carbon dioxide emissions.

The Biological Diversity Treaty proposed to protect plant and animal life did not fare much better. The United States refused to even sign the treaty because of a clause that would allow governments to share with corporations in the profits gained from goods taken out of their forests and natural wildlife habitats. Although 158 other nations did sign the treaty, 100,000 species were extinguished between the years of 1992 and 1997.

World leaders attending the Earth Summit could not even agree on a forest treaty and instead settled on 15 nonbinding forest principles. Although the United Nations has announced 135 proposals for action, tropical forests continue to shrink rapidly, especially in Brazil, Indonesia, Mexico, and Venezuela.

Although that first Earth Summit held in Rio de Janeiro years ago did lead to the creation of hundreds of environmental agencies and numerous environmental conventions, and an Earth Summit II brought together world leaders once again to address all imaginable aspects of sustainable development, Dr. Jones contends that the year 1992 did not live up to its promise. According to his well-received lecture, the only thing that can ensure the survival of the planet and its inhabitants is the creation of a single, legally-binding document signed by all nations. Dr. Jones suggests world leaders leave their politics, their economics, and their approval rating statistics at home for Earth Summit III so they can get serious about saving the world.

Global Agreements

Discuss the following questions based on the student reading with others in your class.

1. Environmental concerns constitute a global issue. Greenhouse gas emissions reductions in one or two nations (or even 10 or 20) will not curb global warming trends if other nations continue to pollute the air with carbon dioxide from car exhausts. Water contamination does not stop at national borders. Yet our world is divided into nations that do not all share the same economic and political ideologies. Is it realistic to assume that a single, legally binding document about anything would ever be signed by all nations of the world as Dr. Jones hopes?

2. Financing the strategies devised to promote sustainable development—the improvement of human conditions in the absence of environmental degradation—was discussed at both Earth Summit meetings of governmental leaders. Since developing countries do not have the finances to manage such changes, developed countries have committed anywhere from .27% to .7% of their Gross National Products to a fund called Official Development Assistance, but no clear-cut levying system has yet been established. How might it best be decided which countries should provide monies to the ODA, and at what level should each contributing country be expected to contribute?

3. It has been suggested by some environmentalists that contributing to the ODA is more a matter of self-interest for a nation than of altruism. What might be meant by this statement?

4. Oil companies, certain government officials, and even some scientists suggest that the concerns about global warming, ozone layer depletion, and animal endangerment are exaggerated. They suggest that computer models and scientific predictions can only be so accurate. They also contend that climate changes are affected more by natural fluctuations than by human activity. What purpose would scientists have to exaggerate their claims that human activity is affecting the global environment in negative ways? Why would oil companies in particular wish to downplay environmental concerns? Even if scientific predictions about global warming, population growth, and ozone layer depletion prove sometime in the future to have been exaggerated, why would it be prudent to heed their concerns in the present?

5. Do you think reducing greenhouse gas emissions below 1990 levels can be achieved in the United States? Would reducing gas emissions create noticeable economic or social changes? What personal lifestyle changes would need to take place to reduce emissions? How would transportation have to change? How might such changes be regulated?

Forestalling Disaster

On November 18, 1992, the Union of Concerned Scientists released a document entitled *Warning to Humanity*. The paper, which was signed by the majority of the world's Nobel Laureate prize winners in the sciences and over 1,500 members of scientific academies from 69 nations throughout the world, begins with the words, "Human beings and the natural world are on a collision course." The document highlights critical stresses on the environment and urges government officials, industrial and religious leaders, and all people of the world to work together to save the earth. Match the environmental stresses listed in the box with their causes and consequences described below.

ENVIRONMENTAL STRESSES

Ozone layer depletion	Ground water depletion	Ocean degradation
Loss of soil productivity	Deforestation	Species extinction
Global warming	Overpopulation	Air pollution

CAUSES AND CONSEQUENCES

1. This increase in the earth's temperature is caused by a buildup of "greenhouse gases," including carbon dioxide. Due to the burning of fossil fuels and the destruction of forests, global temperatures are expected to rise about 2 degrees Celsius over the next century. (The global temperature during the last ice age was only 2.2 degrees Celsius lower than it is today.) Predicted consequences include a rise in sea levels, coastal flooding, growing-season changes, major climatic pattern changes, and desertification.
   Environmental Stress: _____

2. The world's population is not expected to stop growing until it has nearly tripled today's 5.4 billion mark. The consequences of this growth include more pollution, more destroyed habitats, and the consumption of more natural resources.
   Environmental Stress: _____

3. This depletion of an atmospheric layer that protects human beings from ultra-violet radiation can be attributed to chemicals used in aerosol sprays and refrigeration. Consequences of this depletion could include a rise in skin cancers and cataracts and a decrease in the effectiveness of human immune systems and the oceans' plankton population.
   Environmental Stress: _____

4. The destruction of forest lands can be attributed to the over-harvesting of trees for the sake of agriculture, ranch land, and construction. When forests are lost, so are animal and plant species that rely on the ecosystem they create.
   Environmental Stress: _____

5. Dam building, wet lands draining for agricultural purposes, and lake and river polluting are three of the causes of this environmental problem. Consequences include the unavailability of safe drinking water for as many as one in every five people on the planet.
   Environmental Stress: _____

6. Current agricultural practices result in this environmental problem, which in turn reduces per capita food production in many parts of the world.
   Environmental Stress: _____

7. Rivers carrying toxic, industrial, agricultural, and municipal wastes have created a situation in which, according to the *Warning to Humanity*, "the total marine catch is now at or above the estimated maximum sustainable yield." The consequences of not addressing this environmental concern could include our inability to rely on the oceans as a food source and the extinction of many marine plant and animal species.
   Environmental Stress: _____

8. This loss in plant and animal life has many causes including indiscriminate hunting practices, the improper disposal of chemical and toxic wastes, and the destruction of rain forests and coral reefs. With each lost species goes the potential of a medical cure or other human benefit the plant or animal could have provided. In addition to its independent benefits, extinguishing plant and animal species also disrupts the complicated web of life that interconnects humans, animals, plants, and the elements.
   Environmental Stress: _____

9. This pollution is caused by the burning of fossil fuels by industry and especially transportation. It results in ozone depletion, acid rain formation, and a number of minor health concerns.
   Environmental Stress: _____

Answer Key

The Code of Hammurabi
Victim Rights   Page 5

1. The difference between retributive and restorative justice lies in the consequences of an offense. Retributive supporters usually favor lengthy prison sentences and sometimes the death penalty, while restorative supporters favor community service, victim reimbursement, and victim-offender confrontation. In theory, retributive justice supporters believe offenders should be punished, and restorative justice supporters believe offenders should make amends with society and reenter it with a better education, a support system, and a better chance. Restorative justice advocates believe their approach to be wiser because it attempts to address the origins of crime, to rehabilitate, and to make whole the damage caused. They also cite numerous studies that suggest current policies are ineffective with nonviolent criminals.

2. Moses claimed the ten commandments were sent from God. In fundamentalist Islamic countries, the holy book of the Koran has the force of law.
The laws in the United States gain their authority from the fact that they are voted on by the people and their representatives and the fact that they must conform to the Constitution.

3. An indictment must be presented to anyone accused of a crime. No one can be tried for the same crime twice. No one can be required to be a witness against himself. No one can "be deprived of life, liberty, or property, without due process of law." Accused have the right to a speedy and public trial by jury, witnesses in their defense, and an attorney. Excessive bail, fines, and cruel and unusual punishments are prohibited.

4. A person who feels a company or individual has not completed a job satisfactorily can take the case to court. Because businesses and professionals realize this is possible, many people pay to insure themselves against such cases. The difference in today's system as opposed to Hammurabi's is that Hammurabi's Code spelled out very specific compensation for specific offenses and failed services.

The Magna Carta
Long Live the Queen   Page 12

1. Some claim social arrangements always tend toward hierarchical arrangements and that human beings like the idea of royalty. Others suggest that kings and queens unite a nation by providing citizens with a common identity.

2. The barons were supported by Scotland's King Alexander II. Even so, England would see another 400 or more years of citizen-sovereign disputes before a constitutional monarchy would be solidly established.

3. Although this is a question of personal opinion, students might recognize that since a president serves as both "governor" and "national symbol," elections and governing become more personal matters in republics in which the ruler must answer to the people more directly and campaigns can get personal and unkind.

4. Advantages—A constant constitution gives a strong historical reference—an ultimate place to look in determining the legality of a matter. Being difficult to change gives a constitution stability.
Disadvantages—The world changes and it is impossible to accurately interpret the intent of the original framers of the constitution. Matters arise in the modern world that are not directly addressed in the constitution as they refer to discoveries, inventions, and social systems that did not exist 200 years ago.

The Great Charter   Page 13

1. No government official who represented the king was to demand that a citizen give up any goods for use by the official or others in the government. The king had to pay for anything he, or a representative, took from a citizen.

2. This statement protected the rights to free trade with other nations.

3. This statement gave citizens the right to vote on taxes except in certain cases including the need for ransom money for the king and other specific incidents spelled out in the Magna Carta.

4. This statement assured that citizens accused of a crime would receive a fair trial.

5. This statement assured that punishments fit the crime.

6. This statement assured that a king could not demand more money of a baron or knight than was set forth by law.

7. This statement assured that a citizen did not have to go to the king with a grievance, but that a courthouse would be located in his district.

Presidents, Sultans, Tyrants, and Queens
     Page 14

Part A	Part B
1. c	7. i
2. d	8. g
3. b	9. j
4. e	10. h
5. a	
6. f	

The Declaration of Independence
Freeing the World   Page 20

1. The author suggests that forcing democracy on an unwilling, uninterested, or unprepared nation leads to instability, anarchy, or violence.

2. Students' answers will vary.

3. Many developing countries endure difficult elections—ballot boxes are stuffed, some

candidates are suppressed from running, and military personnel must oversee the entire election process. The fairness of such elections is always in question.

4. Foreign affairs officials probably take into account political, economic, and geographic concerns in determining where to step in. Ally nations secure support as do nations rich in oil and natural resources or in geographically strategic positions. At times, war atrocities overrule all other concerns and the United States, the United Nations, and other concerned nations from around the globe mediate an end to an especially bloody conflict.

5. Students living in a nondemocratic nation may notice less day-to-day differences and more state-of-mind differences. They may feel afraid at all times to act and speak naturally, being aware that speaking against the government or practicing certain religions can land a person in jail in some countries. A citizen in a nation ruled by a military leader must also be prepared for war and/or a whole new set of laws as rulers in such circumstances are toppled and replaced often.

6. Political leaders in countries that exercise majority rule sometimes feel tied down by the majority opinion. They will seldom attempt reforms that are not likely to fare well in the opinion polls, for example. Minority groups (such as blacks and women before the 1960s in America) in a majority rule country sometimes find themselves legally oppressed by unjust laws voted into being by the majority.

A Royal Response   **Page 25**
1. King's Possible Response: Because you are a colony of Great Britain, and I am the sovereign power of that nation, it is my right and duty to approve of all laws before they are put into operation.
2. King's Possible Response: I dissolved the Massachusetts legislature because it advocated to each of the 13 colonies active defiance by sending a circular letter suggesting that British goods be boycotted until the Townshend Acts be repealed. A king who allows subjects to disobey acts of Parliament would be a poor king.
3. King's Possible Response: A large number of officers is necessary in America because the colonies are so far away from the motherland that I need representatives to govern for me in my colonies there.
4. King's Possible Response: I keep standing armies in the Americas for the benefit of the colonists. Do you not want someone to protect you from the Indians?
5. King's Possible Response: Although I have limited the exportation of tobacco, rice, and indigo to England and English colonies only, you are still free to trade in grain and flour on non-British markets in the West Indies and in southern Europe.

6. King's Possible Response: The revenue I am raising through taxation of the colonists is to help pay off the 60 million pounds borrowed to fight battles on your soil—the French and Indian Wars.
7. King's Possible Response: It is my right and duty to dictate the laws to my subjects.
8. King's Possible Response: What you perceive to be injuries are nothing more than the rightful duties of a king and his Parliament.

Revolutionary Pursuit   **Page 26**
1. Twenty percent of the white population were active Tories or Loyalists and probably as many more passively opposed the war. Some Loyalists served in the regular British Army and others served in Loyalist units. Loyalists were physically abused, outcast, imprisoned, and even killed. Many fled to New York City where the Board of Associated Loyalists was located, and others went into exile in England, Florida, the Caribbean, or New Brunswick, Canada.
2. Ten Declaration of Independence signers were farmers, 14 were lawyers, 15 were judges, and 10 were merchants. Other signers included physicians, an ironmaster, an educator, an author, and a publisher—with some overlap of signers who claimed more than one occupation.
3. George Washington said, "I take leave of all the employments of public life," although he did not stand true to his word. In 1783 he presided over the Constitutional Convention, and in 1789 he became the first president of the new United States of America.
4. Benedict Arnold was a distinguished military man in both the French and Indian Wars and the American Revolution until 1780 when he agreed to surrender West Point to the British in exchange for money and a royal commission in the British Army. Angry at his treatment by the Continental Army, and in need of money, he expected to find his needs met with the British, but he died in 1801 as a man distrusted and disliked by two nations.
5. Jefferson wrote that men were endowed with "inalienable" rights, but the final copy reads "unalienable" rights even today.
6. The fighting of the American Revolution started first, on April 19, 1775. Lexington and Concord saw casualties on both sides as the British attempted to seize munitions from colonial minutemen. The second Continental Congress met on May 10, 1775. A resolution for independence was passed on July 2, 1776. All fighting done before that date was done by British rebels who still hoped for reunion with the king, and not by U.S. citizens.
7. Thomas Jefferson called the changes Congress instituted "deplorable" and was especially disappointed that a statement condemning King George and the British people for encouraging the slave trade was not included in the adopted form of the Declaration of Independence.

8. George Washington never fought on the side of the British in the American Revolution, but he did in the French and Indian Wars in which he served as a ranking military officer on the side of the British.
9. Over 200,000 fought on the side of the Patriots during the American Revolution, most being untrained men who brought their own guns and signed on for short-term duties lasting from a few weeks to a few months.
10. On June 7, 1776, Richard Henry Lee moved that the states declare their independence; John Adams seconded the motion. A committee of five including John Adams, Benjamin Franklin, Robert R. Livingston, and Roger Sherman, and led by Thomas Jefferson was elected to draw up the actual declaration. The Lee-Adams resolution of independence was adopted on July 2, 1776, and the declaration itself was adopted on July 4, 1776.
11. The original copy of the Declaration of Independence, given to John Dunlap for printing, was lost. The declaration that was read aloud to the assembly at Philadelphia was a copy attached to the page in a journal at the Congress. The declaration was then engrossed and signed by those present on July 4, 1776. Some signatures were added at later dates for various reasons. The original engrossed declaration can be found in the National Archives Building in Washington, D.C.
12. No, some individuals signed later. New York delegates were not given the authority to sign on July 4. Two Pennsylvania delegates who did not approve of the declaration were replaced, and their replacements signed at a later date. Delegates who were not present for one reason or another on the fourth also signed later.
13. The last surviving signer of the Declaration of Independence was Charles Carroll who died on November 14, 1832, at the age of 95.
14. Two declaration signers went on to become president: John Adams (1791-1802) and Thomas Jefferson (1801-1809).

United States Constitution
Making a Change   **Page 32**
1. Pros—Professional lobbying groups assure that diverse interests maintain visible representation in Washington, D.C. The groups possess the money to complete research, keep interested members informed, and effect change. The lobbyists become known personalities to politicians, providing a face to go along with a cause. Cons—The presence of professional lobbying groups in Washington, D.C., seems to attest to the fact that it takes money to initiate change in modern politics. The opportunities for bribes and abuses of power increase with the presence of such groups. Public policy is taken a step away from individual citizens by adding a middle man between them and their representatives.
2. While some argue that the powers of Judicial Review are a necessary check on state and federal representatives who pass laws, assuring that no statutes contradict the Constitution, others argue that judges are not elected officials and were not intended to have the wide reaching powers that Judicial Reviews provide.
3. Afraid of the misuse of powers, the Founding Fathers separated government into three branches and created checks on the powers of each branch by the other two branches. Some checks and balances include the following:
   A. The president can veto a bill passed by Congress.
   B. Congress can override a veto.
   C. The executive branch appoints judges to the Supreme Court; the Congress approves the appointments.
   D. The Supreme Court can declare laws passed by Congress unconstitutional.
   E. The president is the head of the Army, but only Congress can declare war.
   F. The president can negotiate treaties with foreign countries, but the Congress must vote them into law.
   G. Congress has the power to impeach a president or a Supreme Court judge.
   H. The courts can declare a president's actions unconstitutional.
   I. Constitutional amendments can override a judicial decision.
4. At the time of the writing of the Constitution, Federalists believed any list of fundamental rights would be dangerously incomplete, allowing for unstated rights to be violated; therefore, they decided not to include a Bill of Rights. When several states demanded a list of individual rights, the Founders were careful to include one that stated that including certain rights did not "disparage others retained by the people" (Amendment 9). In general the Bill of Rights assured the freedom of speech, press, assembly, and religion; the right to bear arms and not have soldiers quartered in homes; several specific rights of persons accused of crimes; and all powers "not delegated to the United States . . . are reserved to the states respectively, or to the people."
5. The amendments have protected and extended the rights of various groups of people (i.e., voting rights for women, the dissolving of slavery) and in many cases have clarified or changed policy or procedures (i.e., defining the electoral college, changing the first day of a president's term). The amendment process is described in Article V of the Constitution and was made somewhat difficult so that the document would remain the "Supreme Law of the Land."
6. Examples of phrases no longer in effect in the United States Constitution include the following:
   A. Several sections of the Constitution that make reference to slavery became obsolete with the passage of the Thirteenth Amendment. These include Article I, Section 2's mention of "three fifths of all other persons," Article I, Section 9's mention of the importation of slaves, and Article IV,

Section 2's claim that slaves cannot escape from slave states into free states and be declared free.

B. Since the members of the House of Representatives is based on population, the numbers specified in Article 1, Section 2 no longer apply.

C. The specifics of electing the president mentioned in Article II, Section 1 no longer apply because of the passage of the Twelfth Amendment.

D. The Eighteenth Amendment was repealed by the Twenty-first.

E. The section of many amendments that states that the article shall be inoperable unless ratified becomes mute once the amendment is ratified.

Framing the Framers   Pages 33 and 34
Frame One—Jonathan Dayton
Frame Two—John Blair
Frame Three—James Madison
Frame Four—Rufus King
Frame Five—Alexander Hamilton
Frame Six—Benjamin Franklin
Frame Seven—Patrick Henry
Frame Eight—Thomas Jefferson
Frame Nine—Elbridge Gerry
Frame Ten—Luther Martin
Frame Eleven—John Hancock
Frame Twelve—Oliver Ellsworth

What Went Wrong?   Page 35
2. Not only was a federal court system not established, but Congress could make laws for states—but not for individuals. These weaknesses made it impossible for the federal government to enforce laws under the Articles of Confederation.

3. States were constantly engaging in tariff wars that made interstate trade a nightmare.

4. Some state governments printed so much money that it became worthless (Rhode Island, especially). The federal government was doing the same thing, and the entire economic situation became messy. Neither state nor Confederate money was trusted and so lacked value.

5. There were no provisions in the Articles of Confederation forcing the states to abide by the terms of the Treaty of Paris, and some states embarrassed the new government by entering into their own agreements with foreign nations.

6. Necessary amendments could not pass the difficult obstacle of ratification by 13 very independently minded states!

A Puzzling Document   Page 36

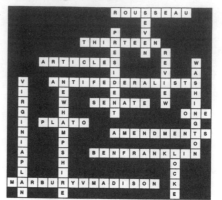

The Bill of Rights
Freedom of Speech   Pages 41 and 42
1. Although this question is based on opinion, students might be informed that some political analysts believe the Founding Fathers were referring to political discourse only when they provided for free speech.

2. Remind students that it is not legally acceptable to exercise your own freedoms to the point of infringing on the freedoms of others.

3. Students may suggest that obscene language infringes on the rights of others.

4. Answer varies from school to school.

5. Although it provides a standard, students may note that "clear and present danger" could be interpreted in a variety of ways.

6. Although not spoken words, these acts are political statements and have been upheld as legal expressions by the courts.

7. Student answers will vary.

8. Students may give examples of how one person's completely unrestricted speech could infringe on the rights of another person, could endanger lives, or cause unrest.

Freedom of the Press   Pages 43 and 44
1. Pro of the policy—there is no public interference with court cases. Con of the policy—governments could be more inclined to corruption if no documents can be released without their permission.

2. Student opinion, but students should be aware that libelous writings are illegal.

3. Student answers will vary.

4. Student answers will vary.

5. Publishing things on the Internet is less restricted at this time than publishing things in books since any person can create a home page. E-mail, although directed to a single person or group of people, could be picked up by others, and so some suggest should carry more restrictions than personal letters.

6. Various Internet issues such as these are being decided in the courts on a case-by-case basis at this time.

7. Student answers will vary.

Freedom of Religion   Pages 45 and 46

1. The idea that the church and state must be separate is a modern interpretation of the First Amendment. Actual wording of the amendment does not suggest this must necessarily be so.
2. The church-state separation standard did grow out of a need to determine how to provide freedom of religion to such diverse groups as are now represented in the nation.
3. Student answers will vary.
4. Many countries declare an official religion but still maintain freedom of religion. It would not happen in the United States because "no law respecting the establishment of a religion" suggests there will be no official state religion.
5. There is no law stating that a student cannot pray in school. The only outlawed prayers are school mandated prayers.

I Know My Rights   Page 48

A. 2   E. 5
B. 4   F. 1
C. 6   G. 8
D. 1   H. 10
               I. 9

The Standard in Human Rights   Page 49

A. Q-L   P. E-R
D. K-I   S. W-AA
G. B-O   V. Z-U
J. H-C   Y. T X
M. N-F

Emancipation Proclamation
Perspectives on the Proclamation   Page 56

1.A. Defining the Civil War as a fight against slavery would dissuade European support of the Confederates.
  B. Timing the publicizing of the Proclamation following a Union victory would boost army morale and raise the Northern opinion of the conflict.
  C. The Proclamation would provide the Union Army with former slaves to serve as soldiers.
2. At the beginning of this nation, citizens identified with their state much more strongly than with their nation. A Virginian was a Virginian first and an American second. Therefore, when the national government blatantly opposed the institution of slavery upon which the Southern states' economy depended by electing an anti-slavery president, they felt it their right to secede—just as Thomas Jefferson stated in the Declaration of Independence, "When in the Course of human Events, it becomes necessary for one People to dissolve the Political Bands which have connected them with another . . ."
However, the 1869 Supreme Court case of *Texas* v. *White* declared secession from the Union unconstitutional, and no state has seriously attempted it since.
3. The Emancipation Proclamation freed "all persons held as slaves within any state, or designated part of a state, the people whereof shall then be in rebellion against the United

States," with the exception of persons in regions already under Union control. The Thirteenth Amendment freed all other slaves of the nation.
4. Lincoln was so easily elected only because of a division in the Democratic party. Acts, compromises, and court cases including the Missouri Compromise, the Compromise of 1850, the Kansas-Nebraska Act, the Dred Scott Case, and the Fugitive Slave Laws were fresh reminders to Lincoln that the issues surrounding slavery were delicate ones. Lincoln probably sensed that any lasting act completely outlawing slavery would have to follow the restoration of a nation divided.
5. The Emancipation Proclamation turned the tide on the slavery issue. It made possible the Thirteenth Amendment, the Republicans' attempts to establish the freed slaves in society, and eventually, the *Brown* v. *Board of Education* decision in 1954, the Civil Rights Movement of the 1960s, and today's continued struggle for equality for all U.S. citizens.
6. Student answers will vary.

I Didn't Know That!   Page 59

1. False. The amendment process does not involve the president, but President Lincoln nevertheless chose to approve the Fourteenth Amendment abolishing slavery which he proposed in his 1864 reelection campaign.
2. True (sort of). President Lincoln claimed the power to seize an enemy's property in times of war as the legal basis of the Emancipation Proclamation.
3. True. Because the North's economy was based on international trade rather than the farming of cash crops, the Northern states depended on the central government to control the national currency and build the roads, bridges, and railways needed to transport goods to the New England ports.
4. False (mostly). John Brown and his followers did raid a federal arsenal, but for a very different reason. Being radical abolitionists, they did not recognize the validity of any laws pertaining to slavery and so attempted to march into the South and free the slaves by force. He was viewed as a martyr by the North when he was tried and executed for his crime.
5. True. In his last few days in office, President James Buchanan made this claim. Even Lincoln at first hoped for a peaceful reuniting of the North and South although he never acknowledged the legitimacy of secession.
6. False (for the most part). Although Northern army generals sometimes set aside captured or abandoned lands for former slaves throughout the four years of fighting, most property was returned to original owners during the Reconstruction years that followed the war, much to the dismay of radical republicans.

7. True and false. President Andrew Johnson fought with Congress continuously over where the powers of the presidency end and those of the Congress begin. His views favoring leniency toward rebels and no assistance to freed slaves angered republicans to the point that they refused to acknowledge Southern state governments set up under Johnson's Reconstruction plans. In February of 1868 impeachment charges were brought against President Johnson on violations of the Tenure of Office Act. The Congress' vote in May of that year fell one vote short of the two-thirds needed to convict him, however, so Johnson remained in office—and continued to fight with Congress—until his term ended the following year.

8. True. Although declared unconstitutional in 1883, the Civil Rights Act barring discrimination by hotels, theaters, and railroads was passed by Congress in 1883.

9. False. The Southern states sent 2 black senators and 14 black representatives to Washington during the Reconstruction years when Carpetbaggers (Northern republicans) and scalawags (Southern whites who supported Reconstruction) ran the South. Blacks filled many state and local offices as well.

10. False (quite the opposite). Republicans, who first took control of the South following the war, created the Freedmen's Bureau and attempted to establish a free economy and a republican form of government based on equality in the Southern states. Then the Reconstruction politicians who were believed to be corrupt were voted out of office and replaced by democrats who passed laws establishing segregation and opposing equality for blacks. Not until the mid twentieth century did some of these laws begin to erode.

11. True. On March 13, 1862, the federal government prohibited Union army officers from returning runaway slaves to the South. The Emancipation Proclamation officially welcomed slaves into the Union Army. By the end of the war, the Union had relied on the services of 186,000 black soldiers, most of whom served in all black units. Twenty-three of these black soldiers were awarded the Medal of Honor for bravery.

12. False. The NAACP, aware that segregation, prejudice and racial hatred, and discriminatory laws and practices continued to enslave blacks as the Emancipation Proclamation centennial approached, began to use the motto "Free by '63" to focus attention on the civil rights movement which was then building momentum.

And the March Goes On   Page 60

1.	F	6.	H
2.	E	7.	D
3.	A	8.	C
4.	G	9.	I
5.	B		

The Communist Manifesto
Marxism for Democrats   Page 66

1. The expansion of trade and industrial expansion created a class of capitalists who profited from the work of the proletarians.

2. The owners of the means of production in a capitalist society possess not only the majority of the money but also a great deal of political and social clout. A true democracy, according to Marx, allows all citizens to share in the decision making regarding how products and profits will be used.

3. The conventional definition of communism focuses on state control of social, economic, and political conditions of the masses. Marxist communism puts all control in the hands of the people.

4. Plank One—The government subsidizes low income housing. It also regulates and/or operates some industries including banks, mass transit, police and fire departments, the postal service, and the military.
   Plank Two—In 1913 the Sixteenth Amendment allowed for the United States to have an income tax. Originally minimal, the income tax takes about a 20% from middle class Americans' paychecks today.
   Plank Three—Inheritances have not been abolished but are taxed at the state and federal levels.
   Plank Four—Paychecks can be garnished in certain cases. Property involved in criminal activities can be confiscated.
   Plank Five—Banks are regulated by a federal insurance and policies system. The Federal Reserve System serves as a bank to commercial banks.
   Plank Six—The Federal Communications Commission regulates communications nationwide and an Interstate Highway System centralizes transportation.
   Plank Seven—Government aid to farmers is about the closest we come to government owned factories, although many utilities have quasi-public ownership.
   Plank Eight—There are no good examples in the United States.
   Plank Nine—City and country populations fluctuate with social and economic condition changes.
   Plank Ten—State and local governments regulate and finance public schools.

5. Nationalism divides workers insofar as workers identify with fellow citizens (workers and capitalists) rather than with fellow workers worldwide. Capitalism creates an overt system of competition for employment and sales wherein a worker must promote his or her own skills over those of other workers rather than cooperating with others having similar abilities.

6. When a corporation owns the means of production, the individuals doing the work are not the individuals making the bulk of the money or the decisions as to how products or profits will be used. This differs greatly from a worker owning his own tools and producing products and/or profits for himself or herself.

Will Work for Profit — Page 67

1. T
2. F—The zenith of capitalism was reached late in the nineteenth century at the height of the Industrial Revolution and before World War I and the new era of communism in Eastern Europe.
3. F—Adam Smith first wrote of capitalism in his 1776 classic, *An Inquiry into the Nature and Causes of the Wealth of Nations*.
4. T
5. T
6. T
7. T
8. F—The capitalist system thrives on surplus monies being pumped back into the production of more goods that will generate more profits and so on.
9. F—Traditional capitalists believe the processes of competition and supply and demand will best dictate a nation's economy. They want very little government interference.
10. F—Capitalism thrives on competition which is why anti-trust laws curb monopolies and limit the powers of giant corporations.
11. T—Although "boom and bust" cycles do plague capitalist systems, legislation such as FDR's New Deal laws and governmental increases and decreases in spending to offset private spending habits help control this problem in modern times.
12. F—Many European countries lean more toward socialism, and even the United States maintains government regulations to protect against capitalist excesses.

Communal Living — Pages 68 and 69
Communes That Continue to Exist

Hutterian Brethren have been around for 450 years. The Hutterites today number over 20,000.

Amish communities have survived 300 years so far. Over 80,000 Old Order Amish continue to dress in black and drive the horse and buggy today.

Monastic Orders have been around at least since the start of Buddhism around 550 B.C. and continue to thrive today. Two of the most prominent Western Christian monastic orders today are the Benedictine and the Cistercian orders.

Communes No Longer in Existence

Shakers were around for 230 years; only a few members still survived in 1980. There remains no substantial settlement of members.

After 32 years the **Oneida Community** abandoned its utopian communist principles and became a joint-stock company. It still exists in this form and is famous for its manufacture of sterling silverware.

Morning Star Ranch welcomed short- and long-term campers from the spring of 1966 until October of 1967 when the growing pressure from neighbors, the Health Department, the Border Patrol—which claimed jurisdiction because the ranch was only seven miles from the ocean—and the Sheriff's Department closed it down. Gottlieb was obliged to citizen arrest the last 14 residents for trespass to

avoid paying substantial fines if they stayed.

Fruitlands lasted for seven and a half months at which time one of its founders joined the Shakers and the other was bankrupted. Interestingly, the bankrupt partner's daughter, Louisa May Alcott, wrote *Little Women*—a book which became a classic—in hopes of making money for her family.

New Harmony reverted to individual ownership of small farms and property after two years. Owen had lost a fortune on the experiment about which he had bragged to President Andrew Jackson of the United States and Queen Victoria of England.

Socio-Economic Alternatives — Page 71

1. B
2. D
3. C
4. F
5. A
6. E
7. H
8. G

The New Deal Legislation
Reviewing the Review — Page 77

1. This is a question of personal opinion, but "excesses of capitalism" refers to the fact that in a system based on competition, there will necessarily be "losers" as well as "winners." When a single person gets "the job," the other ten or one hundred applicants do not get it. One person's earning ten million dollars depends on the physical labors of thousands of workers. Government regulations and the welfare system were established in an attempt to even out the playing field.
2. Although a level of poverty probably always exists, the face of poverty changes with changes in socio-economic conditions. Before the Industrial Revolution most Americans lived on farms or in small towns, rather than in big cities. Many extended family members lived together for life. "Nonessential" products were not demanded or even produced. Single parent households were almost unheard of. These different conditions meant that even "poor" citizens could likely get along without federal financial assistance.
3. Roosevelt's New Deal programs have been categorized as policies to promote relief, recovery, and reform. Reform legislation such as the Social Security Act and the establishment of the Federal Deposit Insurance Corporation and the Securities and Exchange Commission were certainly intended to continue into the future, but farm subsidies, government loans, and work programs were much more likely to have been viewed by Roosevelt as temporary relief recovery measures intended to restore economic health to the nation.
4. This question has yet to find an answer even among government officials and advocates for the poor. Students will voice personal opinions in attempting to devise a system of welfare reform that does not pit poor against poor.
5. The framers of the Constitution clearly did not intend for citizens to be in want of food or shelter, but there exist no specific provisions within the document to ensure this will not happen.

6. Student answers will vary.
7. Student answers will vary based on individual interpretations of the religion clause of the First Amendment. Pros of church welfare systems include the potential for a more personal and caring approach to the problem of poverty. Cons include the lack of accountability when the government has no direct involvement in how its welfare money is spent and the fact that the church-state division becomes murky.

What's Left of the New Deal?   **Page 78**
1. O.
2. O.—Also known as the Wagner Act, it was limited in scope by the Taft-Hartley Act of 1947, but it marked a clear change in attitude for the federal government.
3. O.—Now titled the Social Security Administration, this agency has expanded a great deal since 1935.
4. N.O.—This act was declared unconstitutional in 1936, but a second Agricultural Adjustment Act soon followed.
5. N.O.—Although only in operation for ten years, some of this agency's functions have since been assumed by the General Services Administration.
6. O.
7. O.—Today the administration guarantees bank loans to finance large, rural projects.
8. N.O.—Codes devised by the National Recovery Administration were declared unconstitutional and are no longer in effect.
9. O.— Although New Deal legislation expanded aid to children and developed it into a state-federal joint project, the Illinois legislation was passed 20 years earlier in 1911.
10. N.O.—Congress abolished the corps in 1942.

Rules and Regulations   **Page 79**
1. Federal Communications Commission
2. Food and Drug Administration
3. Environmental Protection Agency
4. National Highway Traffic Safety Administration
5. Consumer Product Safety Commission
6. Nuclear Regulatory Commission
7. Federal Trade Commission
8. Federal Reserve Board
9. National Labor Relations Board
10. Antitrust Division of the Justice Department
11. Securities and Exchange Commission
12. Occupational Safety and Health Administration

Putting It in Perspective   **Page 80**
Oct. 29, 1929—D. Stock market crash
March 4, 1933—E. F.D.R. inaugural speech
March 9-June 16, 1933—J. First Hundred Days
August 14, 1935—C. Social Security Act
June 28, 1938—I. Minimum wage
August 2, 1939—G. Einstein letter
September 3, 1939—A. World War II begins
August 14, 1941—M. Atlantic Charter signing
December 7, 1941—F. Pearl Harbor attack

December 8, 1941—K. U.S. enters World War II
April 12, 1945—B. F.D.R. dies
May 7, 1945—H. Germany surrenders
August 6 and 9, 1945—L. Hiroshima and Nagasaki bombed
August 15, 1945—N. Japan surrenders

The Civil Rights Act of 1964
Grandpa's Wisdom   **Page 87**
1. Evidence that "outsiders" have not yet realized true equality can be found more in testimonials and statistics than in the law. Although most federal, state, and local laws forbid discrimination, statistically women are paid less in the business world and hold few upper management positions, minorities make up a portion of the prison population far greater than their numbers in the general population justify, and homosexual couples are given dubious reasons for not being accepted into apartment complexes. Students may suggest that the civil rights movement is over since no legislation as significant as the Civil Rights Act has been initiated since the sixties, or they may cite gay parades, affirmative action debates, and the abortion debate as evidence that the struggle for civil rights continues today.
2. Black culture grew in the 1920s as African Americans became urbanized and established their own newspapers, magazines, jazz music clubs, and political organizations; but still the average black man worked in a factory or on a farm, felt the fear that legal lynchings can bring (1,000 blacks were lynched in the year 1890), and were kept from voting because of poll taxes and literacy test requirements. During the Great Depression, many blacks were poor and unemployed. Some New Deal policies were influenced by an informal "Black Cabinet," but other policies excluded blacks in their terms. The Social Security Act, for example, excluded 65% of working blacks by not including domestics or farmers. Blacks in the fifties gained support from some whites for a growing movement for equality but continued to experience segregation and discrimination in everyday life. Blacks today are approaching equality but continue to be confronted with social and economic inequality. Black women experienced many of the same things as black men over the years but were not—until recently—well represented in the business world. Women of all colors were not given the vote until 1920 and continue to battle social and economic discrimination today.
3. Answers will vary.
4. Answers will vary, but some examples are contained in the answer to question #1.
5. A. The *Plessy* v. *Ferguson* case prompts establishment of civil rights organizations.
   B. NAACP fights to end lynching laws and segregation policies.
   C. *The Crisis* points out unfair treatment of black soldiers in World War I.
   D. Both world wars lead to the increased urbanization of blacks.

E. Philip Randolph's threatened march on Washington procures equal hiring of blacks by contracted war industries and eventual desegregation of U.S. armed forces.

F. Thurgood Marshall wins *Brown* v. *Board of Education*.

G. Rosa Parks is arrested when she refuses to give up her seat on the bus.

H. Sit-ins, marches, and protests are organized and carried out with varying success.

I. Martin Luther King, Jr., gives his "I Have a Dream" speech as part of the March on Washington.

J. Martin Luther King, Jr., turns to issues of poverty before his assassination.

K. The rich continue to hold the political clout in the nation.

6. Answers will vary.

The Jury Is Still Out   Pages 88–91

These case scenarios will be decided by personal interpretations of the Civil Rights Act, but a few interesting points are provided here.

1. Although Title VI does not mention sex, a 1991 amendment to the act does, making it illegal to deny the benefit of a sports team to girls in this case since public schools are federally funded.

2. Title II states that all persons shall enjoy the "full and equal enjoyment of services and goods," but the courts have made no clear decisions about whether an exclusive religious or ethnic club is discriminatory.

3. Although Affirmative Action cases have suggested that a company can have a general goal of hiring more minorities (including women), specific cases cannot discriminate under Title VII.

4. Title I assures that no voting qualification tests can determine one's eligibility to vote. Transient citizens can register to vote as long as they list a place of residence (i.e., under the bridge on Fourth Street) so that their precinct can be determined. Because voter registration must take place at least 20 days before one is allowed to participate in an election, many homeless people have moved on and do not show up to vote.

5. Title V specifically states that no procedure must be followed that is not explicitly defined in the federal register.

6. Churches, being private institutions, are not covered under the Civil Rights Act.

7. This is not directly addressed in the act. Students should justify opinions.

8. Title II deems it illegal to "intimidate, threaten, or coerce" in an attempt to withhold rights and services.

9. Although not specifically outlawed by any title of the Civil Rights Act, there is mounting multicultural pressure against such situations.

10. Title VII addresses employment issues. Unless it can be proven that the company operates under discriminatory promoting policies, it can probably not get in trouble for a lack of minorities in high positions.

11. Title IV states that "the assignment of students to public schools in order to overcome racial imbalances" does not fall under the definition of desegregation.

A Newcomer's Welcome   Pages 92 and 93

Students will use their own judgments to decide which policies are discriminatory, but they should be able to justify their responses.

Alphabet Soup   Pages 94–96

1. Peaceful Civil Disobedience, Litigate and Legislate, Educate the Public
2. Peaceful Civil Disobedience
3. Started out with Peaceful Civil Disobedience, moved to Litigate and Legislate and finally to Violent Activities
4. Educate the Public, Litigate and Legislate
5. Educate the Public, Litigate and Legislate
6. Educate the Public, Peaceful Civil Disobedience
7. Violent Activities, Litigate and Legislate, Educate the Public, Civil Disobedience
8. Violent Activities
9. Litigate and Legislate, Educate the Public
10. Violent Activities

The United Nations Charter

U.N. Dues Are Due   Page 102

1. Students might mention that the problem with five permanent seats is that world powers sometimes shift and suggest a need for additional "permanent" seats such as some have suggested be added for Germany and Japan. They also may note that political adversaries sometimes abuse the veto power as a means of "snubbing" enemies rather than focusing on the peace issue at stake.

2. The United States may have such high dues because of our influential position in the world as well as our country's wealth. Whether or not this is fair is merely student opinion.

3. Making general assembly resolutions enforceable would move the United Nations toward becoming a world government rather than a forum for discussion among governments. Student opinion dictates whether that would be a good or bad thing.

4. Enforcing World Court decisions would give the court more authority but again would move the United Nations toward being a world government.

   A. Students might note that when so many different governmental systems are involved in a single body, operations of the United Nations are sometimes influenced by politics, which may in the case of Bosnia, slow down the criminal tribunal process.

   B. A look at news reports will show that the U.N. is usually effective in protecting citizens, usually effective in providing humanitarian relief, and sometimes effective in initiating the negotiating process.

   C. Sometimes U.N. resolutions are ignored by world leaders, but those resolutions that receive the backing of more powerful countries usually receive the backing of the world.

Charter of the United Classroom
Pages 103 and 104
An example of a class charter follows:
We the students of Ms. Smith's class are determined
- to establish a precedent of respect, responsibility, and intellectual pursuit that future eighth grade classes can admire and endeavor to uphold, and
- to promote human rights and dignity for all students in the class, and
- to maintain justice and respect for classroom rules and procedures, and
- to offer suggestions for an improved learning environment for all
And will attempt
- to live and work together as good neighbors, and
- to unite our strengths in peacefully conducted groups, and
- to never resort to physical fights or name calling in resolving disputes, and
- to work together for the betterment of all classmates

We hope to accomplish these aims with the agreement of all students and the help and support of our teachers and administrators.

Charting the Charter   Pages 105 and 106

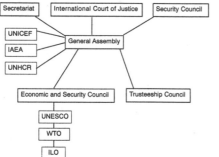

The Earth Summit Agreements
Global Agreements   Page 112
1. Student opinion will dictate the answer to this question, but recent difficulties suggest that legally binding agreements between all nations of the world are not likely. In the absence of an effective world court or global checks and balances of any kind, there is no accountability or incentive for nations to cooperate.
2. An indisputable policy defining which countries will contribute to the ODAS and to what degree would expedite compliance with global agreements on environmental policy reform.

3. Because environmental concerns do not recognize national boundaries, it is in a given nation's own best interest to assist less economically sound countries to comply with international environmental improvement agreements.
4. Oil companies not wishing to pay for expensive new pollution control technologies or to lose business are likely to downplay the role of human activity in global warming and ozone layer depletion whereas scientists have no motive for issuing exaggerated claims. By the time evidence is indisputable, it will be too late for corrective action; consequently, it would be prudent to heed recent warnings.
5. Reducing greenhouse gas emissions would require a major shift in transportation means in this country. That in turn would likely lead to the development of self-sufficient, small communities in which houses, stores, and offices are all located within walking distance for the community's members. In addition to major transportation shifts, alternative forms of energy would need to replace or at least supplement the use of electricity.
6. Industrial leaders who focus on producing and making money are not as interested in environmental concerns as scientists and environmentalists. Government leaders are in the difficult position of attempting to appease voters, to maintain successful national economies, and to acknowledge scientifically supported environmental concerns that could affect not just their citizens, but the entire world. Therefore, some NGO's (nongovernmental organizations) have banned together in the belief that individual groups and citizens who share concerns about the environment are in the best position to effect change. Others advocate the creation of a democratically elected United Nations' environmental decision-making board that would not be forced to await agreement of all nations on environmental issues of concern.

Forestalling Disaster   Page 113 and 114
1. Global warming
2. Overpopulation
3. Ozone layer depletion
4. Deforestation
5. Ground water depletion
6. Loss of soil productivity
7. Ocean degradation
8. Species extinction
9. Air pollution